JOHN WESLEY

THE MAN, HIS MISSION AND HIS MESSAGE

DAVID MALCOLM BENNETT

rhiza press

John Wesley: The Man, His Mission and His Message
Copyright © David Malcolm Bennett 2015
Published by Rhiza Press
www.rhizapress.com.au
PO Box 1519, Capalaba Qld 4157

National Library of Australia Cataloguing-in-Publication entry
Creator: Bennett, David (David Malcolm), 1942- author.
Title: John Wesley: the man, his mission and his message / David
Malcolm Bennett.
ISBN: 9781925139273 (paperback)
Subjects: Wesley, John, 1703-1791.
        Methodist Church--Clergy--Biography.
        Methodists--Biography
        Methodism--History.
Dewey Number: 287.1092

Dedication

This book is dedicated to my patient wife, Claire, who, like me, began life in a Methodist family.

CONTENTS

NOTES

The claimed attendance figures at the open-air preaching of John Wesley and George Whitefield are often doubted; they reported that, on some occasions, crowds numbering 20,000 or 30,000 listened to their preaching. It is likely that both men overstated the numbers. However, when Whitefield was preaching in America, Benjamin Franklin estimated that a crowd of 25,000 could all hear him speak. There is no doubt that sometimes thousands gathered to hear the two great preachers. It is my judgement that their estimates were not likely to be more than double the actual figure, and may have been closer than that. I have generally quoted the numbers that they gave. Halve those figures if you wish.

Quotations from John Wesley's sermons are from John Wesley, *Forty-Four Sermons* (London: Epworth, [1787] 1944). How much these versions differ from his spoken words is impossible to know, but, for the most part, they are all we have to go on. The printed addresses are probably more formal than the spoken sermons.

Much of the dialogue in this biography is drawn from Wesley's writings and the works of other writers. Some of it, however, I have imagined.

David Bennett (November 2014).

CHAPTER 1

THE DELIVERANCE

The dream was becoming a little too vivid. John could see the flames, hear the crackling and smell the smoke. Why were nightmares so real? It was almost as if the house was really on fire.

It was the shouts of 'Fire! Fire!' that finally woke him. The five-year-old tumbled out of his bed and found himself faced with thick, black smoke. His brother and sisters were nowhere to be seen. He rushed to his bedroom door, which was already ajar, and peered out. The house, his house, was on fire. The smoke was billowing up the staircase into his room and through it the flicker of flames could be seen down below, creeping up the stairs. This was not a dream. The fire was real and John 'Jacky' Wesley was in grave danger.

Outside the house the neighbours, awakened by the noise, were rushing forward with pails of water to try to extinguish the flames. But it was a hopeless task. The flames had too great a hold.

Also outside Rev Samuel Wesley and his wife, Susanna, were gathering their children around them. They counted them. Seven! Seven? One was missing. 'It's Jacky,' Susanna cried. 'Jacky's not here. Where is he?' her voice rising in pitch in panic. Samuel did a hasty recount and clearly one was missing; it was John. Where was he? Surely not still in the house.

The flames were now rapidly ascending, flashing and sparkling as they rose, propelled by a strong wind. The house was clearly lost, but John had to be still inside. How could he be rescued in this inferno? They heard a voice call out from inside, which confirmed he was there.

Samuel went through the front door and tried to reach him, but the fire was too fierce and all-encompassing, so he quickly retreated. He made another attempt, but failed again. Susanna, eight months pregnant and unwell, also tried by another route, but it was impossible to go upstairs because of the flames, so she also turned back. She tried again with the same result. Prayer now seemed the only option, so they prayed for their son's deliverance.

Suddenly, a cry went up from the street. 'There he is! He's at that window. There at the top!' A finger pointed upwards. All eyes followed in that direction and there amidst the billowing smoke, framed in a window, was the tiny figure of John Wesley.

How could he escape? He could jump from the window, but if he did that he would almost certainly hurt himself seriously.

'Come here, Will. Get on my shoulders.' It was Mr Rhodes, one of the neighbours, a tall man of considerable strength, calling to a companion.

Rhodes bent down right below the window, and after Will had climbed upon his shoulders, tentatively rose to a standing position. But Will fell off. They tried again. This time Rhodes was able to stand to his full height and his companion, though unsteady, managed to retain his position. Then Will stretched out his hands to just below the window, behind which the terrified boy stood.

'Reach out to me, Master John. Reach out!'

John Wesley, standing on an old chest, looked down and saw the two unsteady figures, one on top of the other, and the ground beneath. He hesitated. He looked back at the smoke and the flames that had now reached the room behind him. He leaned forward, arms outstretched, and fell into Will's grasp and was lowered to the ground.

A few moments later the roof of the house collapsed inwards, away from the boy and his rescuers. John Wesley had escaped only just in time.

The Wesleys were then all taken into a neighbour's house. As they entered their temporary shelter, Samuel called them to prayer. 'Let us give thanks to God! He has given me all my eight children. Let the house go, I am rich enough.' They then all fell on their knees in prayer. In the days and weeks ahead the family was housed in various homes of relatives and friends while their house was rebuilt.

It was later believed that the fire had been deliberately lit, seemingly by some of Samuel Wesley's parishioners. It appears that they did not like their local Anglican rector's preaching and they did not approve of his politics, and this was their terrible way of exacting revenge.

On that day, 9 February 1709, the house was destroyed, but John Wesley was saved. His later life was spent spreading spiritual fire throughout Britain, and eventually, through his spiritual successors, fire throughout the world.

John Wesley later described himself as 'A brand plucked out of the fire' (Zech 3:2 & Amos 4:11). And so he was.

CHAPTER 2

THE WESLEYS

John Wesley was the fourth son and 15th child of nineteen born to Samuel and Susanna. An earlier son had been named John but had died young. The second John, it would seem, was to fill the gap left by his departed brother.

Samuel Wesley was born in 1662 and went to Exeter College in Oxford. He was ordained as a priest in the Church of England in 1689, though he had been raised as a Dissenter. His father and paternal grandfather had been amongst the 2,000 clergy who had been dismissed from their parishes in the terrible Great Ejection in August 1662, when they refused to submit to the new regime governing the Church of England. This effectively meant no parish, no preaching and no income, at least no income from the ministry. Any attempt at preaching could mean a large fine or imprisonment.

Samuel Wesley served briefly as a naval chaplain, before becoming rector in the parish of South Ormsby in Lincolnshire in 1690 or 91. About five years later, he moved to Epworth in the same county, and the parish of Wroot was added to his responsibilities in 1722. He was a man of considerable intellect and wrote poetry, including a 9,000-line poem on the life of Christ, and the scholarly *Dissertations on the Book of Job*.

His wife, Susanna, though, was probably the more remarkable of the two. Her father was also a clergyman, Samuel Annesley, a determined puritan of high principles and strong will, who became known as 'the St Paul of the Nonconformists'. He was another who had been dismissed in the Great Ejection. This was especially difficult for the Annesley family, as they had over twenty children. Friends were not quite sure how many. Was it 24 or 25? Susanna was one of the youngest of these. She knew what it was like to live in a clergyman's family and knew what it was to be poor. It was as well that she had had those experiences, because her future would be full of ministerial difficulties and financial woes. She decided as a teenager to leave the Dissenters and join the Church of England.

Samuel married Susanna on 11 November 1688; he was 26 and she only 19. She was the taller of the two and had an elegant bearing. He appeared more stiff and formal. Yet though Susanna was rather serious, Samuel tended to be witty and poetic. They seem to have had a genuine love for each other at the beginning, but that wilted as difficulties arose and children were born. Their first child, named after his father, arrived in February 1690. After that they came more or less yearly.

When on one occasion Susanna was delivered of twins, Samuel, with the family's finances in tatters, wrote to his Archbishop thanking him for help to feed his ever-increasing family. 'Last night', he told him, 'my wife brought me a few children. There are but two yet, a boy and a girl. I think they are all at present.' The twins were number 12 and 13 in the brood. They both died in infancy. Of the 19 children born to the Wesleys only ten lived to adulthood, seven girls and three boys.

With frequent confinements and such a large crowd to look after, Susanna did not have much time for herself. In fact, her life became almost totally dedicated to her children, educating them herself, girls as well as boys. When engaged in private prayer in the home, it is said that Susanna threw her apron over her head, so that the children knew not to interrupt her. She was a strict disciplinarian and took special care of her children's religious education. As soon as each child had learned how to speak, Susanna taught them the Lord's Prayer. It was said that she had the knack of teaching in ways that made things easy to remember. The older children were also expected to assist in the Christian instruction of their younger siblings. For example, Emilia, one of John's older sisters, sat down with him each day and helped him read a Psalm and a passage from the New Testament, correcting him when he made an error. Yet with John there were few errors.

Each evening Susanna would speak to and counsel individually one or two of her children, including John on Thursdays and Charles on Saturdays. She recognised that each one was different and each had his or her own specific needs and problems.

She taught them 'to fear the rod and to cry softly. By which means,' she argued, 'they escaped abundance of correction they might otherwise have had'. However, once a child was punished for a misdemeanour that was the end of it. She did not hang the deed over their heads as an on-going threat. She also adopted the practice that if one of her children confessed their fault and promised not to do it again, she did not punish them. This, she thought, taught them to be honest.

Samuel was a strong-willed man. Susanna was an even stronger-willed woman. Samuel had an intense loyalty to the Crown of England, at that time represented by King William III, and it was Samuel's practice to pray for the king during their time of family prayer. But Susanna refused to say 'Amen!' to that particular prayer, for in her opinion William had no right to the throne. Her loyalty was to the line of James II. Samuel was furious about her stand. According to Susanna, he knelt down and prayed that God's judgement should rest on him 'if ever he touched me more or came into bed with me before I had begged God's pardon and his.' Her husband then told her, 'If we have two kings, we must have two beds.'

This resulted in Samuel leaving the family home early in April 1702 to go to London, under the guise of other duties. While there he attended the church's Convocation, but he stayed longer than neces-sary for that. Samuel returned to the family home probably early in September that year. Which of them gave way to settle the dispute is unknown, but it was probably not Susanna. The practical cause for their reunion appears to have been a fire in the rectory. This had caused a lot of damage, making considerable repairs necessary, though it was not as destructive as the later fire mentioned in chapter one. In addition, by then King William was dead, and prayers for his successor, Queen Anne, were not such a divisive issue.

John Wesley was born on 17 June 1703. His brother, Charles, arrived in December 1707. If the two feuding lovers had not come together again, there would have been no John and Charles Wesley and no Methodism.

Samuel Wesley went away again for some months at the end of 1711. While he was away, Susanna led Sunday afternoon devotions for the family, servants and immediate neighbours in their large kitchen. This included her reading from a book of sermons. Other neighbours heard how good these sessions were and invited themselves along. The numbers grew and grew until more attended these afternoon gatherings than attended church on Sunday morning. She estimated that on one Sunday over 200 crowded into the rectory, with more wanting to get in but unable to do so.

The minister substituting for Samuel was not impressed and complained to him about these unorthodox gatherings. An unordained person was preaching, and a woman at that. (Though was she preaching?) Samuel urged his wife to stop holding these meetings, but did not order her to do so. Susanna told her husband:

> If you do, after all, think fit to dissolve this assembly, do not tell me that you desire me to do it, for that will not satisfy my conscience; but send me your positive command, in such full and express terms as may absolve me from all guilt and punishment, for neglecting this opportunity of doing good, when you and I shall appear before the great and awful tribunal of our Lord Jesus Christ.

Samuel did not respond to that and the meetings continued.

The following year smallpox struck the family. Five of the children caught it, including John. His mother said 'Jack has borne his disease bravely, like a man, and indeed like a Christian, without any complaint, though he seemed angry at the smallpox when they were sore, as we guessed by his looking sourly at them, for he never said anything.'

Susanna did not allow her children to eat between meals. This John always obeyed. When offered a snack between meals by a neighbour or friend, he would answer, 'I thank you. I will think of it.' He thought about it but did not eat. Indeed, he thought through everything. His father lamented that, in his opinion, 'Jack would not attend to the most pressing necessities of nature unless he could give a reason for it.'

It would probably be unfair to say that John was the family favourite, but Susanna did view him as a special child because of his deliverance from the fire. She thought that because he only just escaped so terrible a disaster, this must mean that God's hand was upon him. That deliverance must have been of God, therefore God surely had a special ministry for him.

In his early years John Wesley moved mainly in a world of females. When he was aged about one, Samuel, his only older brother, moved away to attend school and Charles was not born until John was four. His father spent most of his time in his study and had far less contact with him than did his mother. John also had five elder sisters and the family had two maids.

Life in the Wesley household was never easy. As Susanna once said in a letter to John, 'your father and I seldom think alike'. Also, with such a large family, Samuel was usually in debt. He even spent time in jail because of his inability to repay one loan, though while there he showed considerable concern for his fellow prisoners. John Wesley learned from this. He feared and hated debt. Years later John, ever the autocrat, told his preachers, 'Contract no debt without my knowledge.'

CHAPTER 3

OXFORD UNIVERSITY AND THE HOLY CLUB

If John Wesley's education began at his mother's knee, it continued at Charterhouse School, which at that time was in London. The environment was not a happy one. Boarding schools were not usually pleasant places and the younger boys often suffered greatly at the hands of the older lads, as well as from the masters. Wesley, who was probably never overfed at home, was on a stringent diet in his early years at Charterhouse, mainly because the senior boys helped themselves to the best food, leaving what they did not want for the younger ones.

His father had advised him to run around the school garden three times each morning. This he did. No doubt this contributed to his fitness, which was still evident well into his old age.

Two decades after he had left school he confessed that at Charterhouse he was 'much more negligent than before, even of outward duties, and almost continually guilty of outward sins,' though not those that were particularly 'scandalous'. At that time he hoped that he would be saved by 'not being so bad as other people, having still a kindness for religion, and by reading the Bible, going to church and saying' his prayers.

At the age of 17, Wesley went to Christ Church College at Oxford. Oxford was a better environment for him. However, he was not against enjoying himself in his early days there. In fact, for a while pleasure may have dominated his life. He played billiards, backgammon and chess, and went to coffee houses, taverns and the races. He also liked the company of young ladies and they liked the charming, good-natured Mr Wesley. Though small in stature, he had a dynamic and attractive personality. In fact, he was very sociable and made friends easily. Betty Kirkham, the sister of a close friend, particularly took his fancy, and she, too, was attracted to him. While he hesitated, worried over his lack of money to support a wife, she married someone else.

Yet as his time at Oxford progressed, he became a good scholar, for he had considerable intelligence, a logical mind and a love of books and learning. He was formidable in debate. He also proved to be gifted in understanding the Bible in its original languages. He had received a good grounding in these languages at Charterhouse.

While at Oxford he read the *Imitation of Christ* by Thomas à Kempis, which had quite an impact upon him. Though he had a high regard for it, in one respect it was not to his liking. 'I can't think', he observed, 'when God sent us into the world He had irreversibly decreed that we should be perpetually miserable in it.'

At Oxford and in later life, Wesley read widely. His diary shows that from 1725-35 he read nearly 700 books, many of them of a theological nature, and he did not just read them, he absorbed them and shared many of them with his friends. These books included Jeremy Taylor's *Holy Living and Holy Dying* and William Law's *A Serious Call to a Devout and Holy Life*. Law's book greatly influenced Wesley in his early days, but he later found it less acceptable.

But his days at Oxford are not best remembered for his abilities as a student or for his ways of enjoying himself. As time progressed, Wesley began to live a disciplined life. He went to bed early and rose early. He prayed regularly, fasted one day each month and did not over-indulge. He made various resolutions, which he wrote down and he re-read them regularly to make sure that he had kept them. He recorded his daily expenditure. All this does not mean that he was excessively austere, but he did live a methodical life.

Like many at Oxford University, Wesley was studying for the

Church of England priesthood, following in his father's footsteps. But he took the process more seriously than many of his fellow students. He graduated in 1724 as a Bachelor of Arts.

In 1726 John Wesley secured a Fellowship at Lincoln College, one of the colleges at Oxford University. There is little doubt that his father pulled some strings to achieve this, but as he had few strings to pull, it can be mostly attributed to the recognition of the young man's own ability. Part of Wesley's responsibilities in his new role was to lecture on New Testament Greek. He became Master of Arts early in 1727 and was ordained in September the following year. He then served as his father's curate in Epworth and Wroot, in which churches he preached regularly.

The parishioners in Wroot seem to have been as stubborn and as antagonistic to the Wesleys as those in Epworth. John's sister, Hetty (who was six years older than him) wrote a poem about the people of Wroot, which ran,

Fortune has fixed thee in a place
Debarred of wisdom, wit, and grace –
High births and virtues equally they scorn,
As asses dull, on dunghills born;
Impervious as the stones their heads are found,
Their rage and hatred steadfast as the ground.

Clearly ministering to these people was not easy.

At about this time John told his parents, 'Leisure and I have taken leave of one another.' As one examines his later life it is clear that he and 'leisure' never became reacquainted. He was always busy and almost seemed to regard an idle moment as a sin.

In 1727 Charles Wesley, following in his brother's footsteps, went to Christ Church, Oxford. Charles was short like John, but a little heavier. When at this time John asked his brother about his religious convictions and practice, Charles answered, 'What, would you make me a saint all at once?' How John answered that, or even if he did, appears to be unknown, but for Charles that process of sanctification took a lot longer. However, it began soon after that exchange, and by early 1729 he was a different man.

Ironically, Charles thought Christ Church anything but a Christian environment. He described it as 'the worst place in the world to begin a reformation in'. Anyone who was serious about religion was ridiculed, and as his faith deepened and developed, the younger Wesley became the object of much scorn. His answer to this was to meet with two like-minded friends for prayer and discussion about religious topics.

In November 1729 John Wesley returned to Oxford, to Lincoln College, and lectured in logic, Greek and philosophy. John also joined the little group that Charles had begun and almost straight away became its leader. The younger brother was used to living in the shadow of his more forceful elder sibling and seems to have accepted the take-over without any ill feelings.

The group grew, though it was never large, and its religious observance, which was already methodical, became even more so under John's leadership. They read the Bible together, prayed together and fasted regularly. They also began to minister to the poor and those in prison. In fact, John Wesley preached in a local prison once a month. In addition, members of this group even paid the debts of some prisoners to gain their release from jail. Inevitably, they attracted the unwanted attention of their irreligious Oxford associates, who, from early on, gave them nicknames, such as Bible Moths, Sacramentarians, the Holy Club and, the one that stuck, Methodists. John Wesley was sometimes even called 'the Father of the Holy Club'.

Yet the members of the group had a high opinion of it and its leader. One paid tribute to Wesley's 'noble endowments of mind' and his 'obliging and desirable conversation', which resulted in many 'pleasant hours' when they met together.

The other famous member of the Holy Club was George Whitefield. In 1732 he went to Oxford and became friendly with the Wesleys, joining them in their religious observances. He proved to be, in some respects, even more remarkable than either of them. However, he was younger with a different background, being born in his family's inn at the end of 1714. He became a Christian while at Oxford, through reading Henry Scougal's *The Life of God within the Soul of Man*. He went on to become the greatest preacher of his age. The lives of John Wesley and George Whitefield were to cross and separate repeatedly over the years ahead, and though their theology disagreed in some respects, which caused friction, their names will always be associated.

CHAPTER 4

GEORGIA

Samuel Wesley died in April 1735. He endured considerable pain during his last days, but John later recorded that his father died experiencing 'the consolations of God'. On his deathbed he said, 'The Christian faith will surely revive in this kingdom. You shall see it, though I shall not.' His three sons tidied up his affairs, which mainly comprised of paying his debts, and in John's case, of completing his father's book on Job. Susanna was still alive and for a time lived with her daughter Emilia and later with her eldest son, Samuel, another clergyman.

In the middle of 1735, John Wesley's mind was on Georgia. The state of Georgia, named after King George II, was the newest of the British colonies in North America. It was in the south-eastern part of that continent and had been founded a little over two years before. The main mover behind the founding of Georgia had been James Oglethorpe. The colony was originally intended partly as a refuge for ex-debtors, the unemployed from Britain and persecuted European Protestants. It was also viewed as a barrier to any Spanish expansion from the south. The initial Georgian settlement was in Savannah, where the Creek tribe of Native Americans proved accepting of the settlers.

It would appear that John Wesley made a quick, perhaps a hasty, decision to go to Georgia to minister to the colony's settlers and the Native Americans. At one stage he was considering filling the vacancy in his father's old parish, but he hesitated and another man was appointed instead. Therefore, with uncertainty hanging over his future, he was approached about going to Georgia by a friend, Dr John Burton of the Society of the Propagation of Christian Knowledge, who was one of the colony's trustees.

'Mr Wesley', Dr Burton said, I understand that you are looking for a ministerial position.'

'Well, yes,' Wesley responded a little guardedly. 'What do you have in mind?'

'Mr Oglethorpe needs two godly men to assist him in the colony of Georgia. He needs a chaplain and a secretary. I thought you would be an excellent choice as the chaplain. I regard you as a proper person for such a position.'

'Chaplain! Is the role just that?'

'You would assist Mr Oglethorpe, of course, but also minister to the other colonists.'

Wesley was slow in replying. 'I will think on it', he said unenthusiastically.

'Well, be quick about it. I must have your answer soon. I'll have to find someone else if you are unavailable.'

'I'll do my best, Dr Burton.'

As it happened, no other suitable positions were available at that time. The thought also occurred to him that he would have opportunity to minister to America's original inhabitants, a prospect that greatly appealed to him. So John Wesley accepted Burton's offer.

On 14 October three vessels left England bound for Georgia. Two carried a total of over 200 settlers and the third was a naval sloop intended to guard them. John Wesley was on one of those ships, named the *Simmonds*. John had persuaded his moody brother, Charles, to apply for and accept the role of Oglethorpe's secretary, so he was also on board. Charles went with confused motives, trying, it would seem, to escape himself. Also on board with them were Benjamin Ingham, a fellow member of the Holy Club, Charles Delammotte, a close associate of John Wesley, and James Oglethorpe.

According to John Wesley, the reason he and his brother were going to Georgia was 'to save our souls'. That is an odd-sounding statement for men already called to preach the Gospel of salvation. But at that time John Wesley viewed the route to salvation as being via personal effort and discipline.

John's time on the *Simmonds* only confirmed that there was something wrong in his spiritual life. On board that ship were 26 German Moravians, men, women and children. The Moravians were a deeply spiritual Christian group, with a strong emphasis on mission. Though Wesley did not know it when the voyage began, those devout Moravians were to challenge his understanding of Christianity significantly.

For Wesley and his companions, life on board the ship was extremely disciplined, as was their usual way. A typical day began with an hour of private prayer from 4 am. This was followed by two hours of studying the Bible and other Christian books together. They then had breakfast at eight. They separated, and after various morning activities, met again at midday 'to give an account' of what they had done that morning and what they intended to do in the following hours. They ate a sparse lunch at 1 pm and then engaged in other practices, often reading to their fellow passengers, some of whom were poor and presumably illiterate. Evening prayers followed at 4 pm and another session of private prayer an hour later. At seven, John attended the Germans' evening service. Sixty minutes later the Wesleys met again with Ingham and Delamotte 'to exhort and instruct one another'. They went to bed between nine and ten. No Christians could have been more dedicated to their faith. No Christians could have been more disciplined.

Their discipline was shattered, their faith dented, during a sequence of frightening storms in January. After one terrifying storm John Wesley recorded how ashamed he was of his 'unwillingness to die'. Six days later, after another storm, he made the same confession. That evening Wesley went to the German service. As they worshipped, an even more terrible storm was unleashed upon them. The sea burst repeatedly over the ship, flooding the decks. The boat plunged wildly. The main sail was torn to shreds. It was terrifying. 'The English' understandably screamed in fear. Yet 'the Germans calmly' continued their service, as if nothing was wrong. The Moravians' serene demeanour in frightening circumstances deeply impressed Wesley.

He later asked one of the Moravians, 'Were you not afraid?'

The mild-mannered man replied, 'I thank God, no.'

'But were not your women and children afraid?'

'No, our women and children are not afraid to die.'

These statements staggered Wesley. He, John Wesley, devout Christian and Church of England minister had been terrified during this ordeal, but these Moravians, even the children, had not been afraid. This was a kind of Christianity that he had not seen before.

On 5 February, 1736 they arrived in the Savannah River and on the next day set foot on American soil for the first time. They all knelt 'down to give thanks' and read from Mark chapter six, the story of Jesus walking on the sea. In that passage Jesus said to his disciples, 'It is I; be not afraid' – a most appropriate message. These new arrivals brought the European community in Savannah up to about 700.

Probably the most significant moments of Wesley's stay in Georgia were unexpected and not directly connected with his mission. They were encounters with the Moravian community in that colony. The Moravians in Savannah included those who had travelled with him in the *Simmonds* and some who had arrived at an earlier date. Wesley became a close friend of the leading figure amongst these German migrants, August Spangenberg.

On the voyage the Moravians had helped Wesley learn German. He had helped them learn English. This now proved to be a useful exchange.

Wesley asked Spangenberg's advice about Christian work. The Moravian leader gave him some unexpected answers. 'Have you the witness within yourself?' he asked. 'Does the Spirit of God bear witness with your spirit that you are a child of God?'

Wesley was stunned by the personal nature of the questions. He did not know how to answer them, for they were outside his experience.

Spangenberg took nothing for granted and continued, 'Do you know Jesus Christ?'

'I know that He is the Saviour of the world.'

'True, but do you know He has saved you?'

'I hope He has died to save me.'

'Do you know yourself?'

Wesley hesitated. 'I do,' he said without conviction. He later confessed in his journal. 'I fear they were vain words'.

On some occasions John Wesley helped teach in the colony's school. At one stage some of the children from the wealthier families laughed at some of the others because they had no shoes. So Wesley went to school barefoot, to identify with the poorest.

Wesley had gone to America with a high view of America's original inhabitants, to whom he intended to minister. His view of them was along the lines of 'the noble savage' idea. Wesley patronisingly thought of them as 'little children, humble, willing to learn, and eager to do the will of God.' However, he soon found that this was not so. The tribesmen of America were every bit as sinful and resistant to the Gospel as the Europeans.

Yet, while in Georgia, he did have one striking encounter with the Chickasaw tribe, some of whom paid a visit to Savannah. Wesley recorded the questions he asked their chief and the remarkable answers he gave.

Q. Do you believe there is One above who is over all things?

A. We believe there are four beloved things above: the clouds, the sun, the clear sky, and He that lives in the clear sky.

Q. Do you believe there is but One that lives in the clear sky?

A. We believe there are Two with Him, Three in all.

Q. Do you think He made the sun and other beloved things?

A. We cannot tell. Who hath seen?

Q. Do you think He made you?

A. We think He made all men at first.

Q. How do you think He made them at first?

A. Out of the ground.

Q. Do you believe He loves you?

A. I do not know. I cannot see Him.

Q. But has He not often saved your life?

A. He has. Many bullets have gone on this side and many on that side, but He would never let them hurt me.

Q. We have a book that tells us many things of the beloved ones above; would you be glad to know them?

A. We have no time now but to fight. If we should ever be at peace, we should be glad to know.

This report may be coloured by Wesley's idealised opinion of these people plus language difficulties, but, as it stands, the similarities in ideas between what the Native American said and biblical teaching are remarkable.

John Wesley's spiritual life at this time was covered by clouds. His love life was no sunnier. In 1725 Wesley had written up a number of principles by which he tried to run his life. Among them were: 'To avoid idleness, freedom with women and high seasoned meats. To resist the very beginnings of lust, not by arguing with, but by thinking no more of it or by immediately going into company.' He also later instructed his preachers, 'Touch no woman. Be as loving as you will, but hold your hands off 'em.' How well he avoided 'freedom with women' might be argued. Indeed, the term itself is ambiguous. We can only wonder whether he always kept his 'hands off 'em'.

However, it is clear that when he entered into close relationships with women they never worked out well. He was charming and delightful company and women were attracted to him, but this was one area in his life where everything seemed to go wrong.

He had probably more than one romantic liaison in England but none of them had worked out. In Georgia he met Sophy Hopkey.

Sophy was eighteen, intelligent and attractive and the niece of the chief magistrate in Savannah. James Oglethorpe thought that she was the ideal match for Wesley. Wesley thought that he might be right. She had been planning to return to England but Wesley persuaded her to stay. After much close contact with her, he began to think of marriage, though he did have some doubts about it. His doubts were, for the most part, not specifically about Sophy. Rather, his main problem was that he felt that a Christian minister should be free of family ties, so that he could serve his people and God more effectively. He asked Ingham and Delamotte and then the Moravian leaders for advice. They all seem to have had some doubts about Sophy and counselled against the marriage. Wesley, after a brief but intense emotional struggle, abandoned all thoughts of marrying her.

The month after this Sophy became engaged to a Mr Williamson, of whom Wesley did not have a high opinion. Four days later Sophy married her new love. This may have been a providential escape for John Wesley.

But the matter did not end there. A little later, Wesley refused to administer the Holy Communion to Sophy Williamson. Wesley had stated that everyone intending to take communion should advise the curate the day before. Sophy had not done this. Wesley also believed that she had committed a sin (the nature of which is unknown), about which she had not repented. Many thought that Wesley was getting his revenge. Yet the ban arose out of the high standards that he set himself and expected others to follow rather than payback. Sophy's husband was furious and took Wesley to court for defaming her character, suing him for £1,000. The court sat, but after a number of stops and starts the case had an inconclusive result and the money was never paid. But all this caused considerable trouble for Wesley and attendances at his church declined significantly.

John Wesley's growing problems meant that he could no longer stay in Georgia. He left in December 1737, having spent less than two years in America. It is debated how successful or, perhaps more accurately, how unsuccessful he was during his stay in Georgia. However, one thing is clear: he later did not view his time there favourably. He did not work enough with the Native Americans to connect with them successfully. He ministered to the officials and the migrants but some rose up against him. In addition, the Sophy Williamson affair had cast doubts about his character. It all did little to suggest that John Wesley was destined to be a great Christian leader.

Charles Wesley's stay in Georgia had been even shorter than his brother's. He fell out with Oglethorpe and left a year earlier than John.

As John Wesley's ship approached England, George Whitefield, already recognised in England as a powerful and popular preacher, was on board another ship on his way to Georgia. Charles Wesley had been scheduled to travel with Whitefield, but sickness made that impossible.

In an unusually dark mood, just before his arrival back in England, John Wesley recorded in his journal, 'I went to America to convert the Indians; but O who shall convert me? Who will deliver me from this evil heart of unbelief?' Whether things were that black might be argued, indeed, he later debated within himself about the veracity of those sentiments. But there is no doubt that at that time he still had a great deal to learn about himself, and more especially about God and His ways.

Wesley arrived back in England on 1 February 1738.

CHAPTER 5

SALVATION THROUGH FAITH IN CHRIST

John Wesley was an Anglican clergyman, but he doubted that he knew the Christ he served. He had been a missionary to the Native Americans, but was only just beginning to grasp the Gospel that he tried to proclaim. It was obvious to him that he needed a deeper understanding of Gospel truths and a new spiritual dynamic. He now suspected that his strict discipline and many good works were never going to make him right with God.

Yet he seems to have been pointing in the right direction. On his first Saturday afternoon back in England he preached in St John's the Evangelist in London from 'If any man is in Christ, he is a new creature' (2 Corinthians 5:17), a text with some striking Gospel truths. It would seem that his preaching was true to the text, for his sermon so deeply offended many in the congregation that he was not allowed to preach there again. Eight days later he preached in St Andrew's, Holborn, where his father had been ordained. Once more he was told not to come back. These were the first of many such bans, and these bans were not enacted by an objection to methods, but an objection to the teaching Wesley was proclaiming.

Yet in spite of that first sermon topic, he still felt himself lost. How could he find the Christ he preached? To resolve that issue he looked again to the Moravians. He had been deeply impressed by them in America and on the long sea voyage to get there, so he sought out some of that faith in England. On 7 February he met with a Dutchman and a small group of Germans Moravians. These Germans had only just arrived in England and Wesley helped find lodging for them.

The leading figure amongst the Germans was Peter Böhler. Wesley eagerly engaged in a string of conversations with him. On one occasion Böhler told him, 'My brother, that philosophy of yours must be purged away.' But Wesley 'understood him not' and his philosophy remained unpurged.

Still confused and unusually unsure of himself, Wesley travelled to Tiverton in south-western England, where his mother was now living with her eldest son, Samuel. Early in March, while there, John received the startling news that his other brother, Charles, 'was dying' of pleurisy in Oxford. He immediately set out for Oxford and when he arrived was relieved to see that the younger Wesley was recovering.

But someone had beaten John Wesley to his brother's bedside. It was Peter Böhler. John Wesley and Böhler took up their conversations once more. Twenty-four hours later Wesley was 'clearly convinced of unbelief, of the want of that faith whereby we alone are saved.' But being convinced of one's unbelief does not save and Wesley's mood was now even blacker.

Not unreasonably, Wesley began to have doubts about whether he should continue preaching. After all, how could he preach if he did not have faith? He asked Peter Böhler what he thought. Böhler confirmed that he should continue preaching.

'But what can I preach?' asked Wesley in desperation.

Böhler was direct. 'Preach faith till you have it, and then because you have it you will preach faith.'

So Wesley did 'preach faith', faith in Christ. He did it formally and informally, in churches and chapels, in prisons and inns, in fact, almost wherever he found himself. But still his words seemed to outstrip his experience. Some found salvation through his preaching but he did not. He once more had doubts, so he turned to his Greek New Testament and earnestly studied it to find the truth. He was desperate. His soul gave him no peace. He had to find the God he knew so much about. He had to experience the salvation that he knew God offered.

John even had an argument with his brother, Charles, about whether conversion was gradual or sudden. By this time he believed that it should be sudden. Charles angrily disagreed.

But John's belief did not help his mood. His depression plunged to its greatest depths during a period of about four days in the middle of May. At that time he found himself unable to read, meditate, sing or pray. It was his lowest time.

He received a letter from Peter Böhler that gave him some hope and was able to preach at St Ann's, Aldersgate on the following Sunday. He once more preached salvation by faith in Christ and afterwards he once more had the doors of a church closed to him. A week later two more churches banned him. But it was not the judgement of his fellow ministers that Wesley feared. Rather, labouring under an intense feeling of guilt for his sins, he became more aware of the judgement of God. It was as if God's sword hung over him.

Release from his fears of God's judgement and feelings of guilt came rather unexpectedly. On the morning of 24 May he opened his Bible and read 'Whereby are given us exceeding great and precious promises: that by these ye might be partakers of the divine nature.' (2 Peter 1:4) In the afternoon he visited St Paul's Cathedral and listened to the anthem 'Out of the deep have I called unto thee, O Lord. Lord, hear my voice.'

That evening he went 'very unwillingly' to a meeting of a Christian group in London's Aldersgate Street. While there, someone read from Martin Luther's Preface to Paul's letter to the Romans.

At about a quarter to nine, the reader arrived at the place where Luther was describing the change that God works in human hearts through faith in Christ. Suddenly, at least it seemed to be suddenly, John Wesley felt his heart 'strangely warmed'. He felt that he did 'trust in Christ, Christ alone for salvation, and an assurance was given' him that Christ had taken away his sins and saved him 'from the law of sin and death'. There were no flashes of lightning. There were no thunderous outbursts. Wesley did not even, it seems, make a conscious decision to embrace anything or anyone. Rather, God had worked a miraculous change in his heart. It was God's work and Wesley knew it.

That miracle had many wide-ranging repercussions, not just in the life of John Wesley, but also in the lives of thousands that he later contacted. Yet in the days immediately after his conversion John Wesley experienced many temptations. It was not plain sailing. It was not all peace. But now he had the inward spiritual dynamic of God Himself to help him deal with those temptations.

Many students of Methodism have tended to see Wesley's heart-warming experience as an important point in his life but not really his conversion. However, while there may not have been a dramatic change in his outward behaviour after that encounter with God, the inner-Wesley did change dramatically. The doubts had gone, a new dynamic filled his being and he was now ready to take on the world. John Wesley, a long-term servant of the church, had now been converted to Christ.

A little over two weeks after his conversion, he preached a sermon in a church in Oxford on salvation by faith, a doctrine he now not only believed but had experienced. This sermon, or a variation of it, was later to become the first entry in his Standard Sermons, and that teaching was to become central to Methodism.

In those early months of 1738 Charles Wesley had also travelled the same tortuous journey as his elder brother, searching for salvation in Christ. He also consulted with Böhler. He also struggled. On 21 May, three days before John, Charles found himself 'at peace with God', rejoicing 'in hope of loving Christ'. Two days later he wrote the hymn:

Where shall my wondering soul begin?
How shall I all to heaven aspire?
A slave redeemed from death and sin,
A brand plucked from eternal fire,
How shall I equal triumphs raise,
Or sing my great deliverer's praise?

Methodism, true Methodism, had arrived.

***

During this time of searching John Wesley had access to a number of societies. That is, little groups of people determined to experience God and to support each other in practising the Christian faith. Some were based in the Church of England, others were not. Some of them existed before Wesley began to preach and he just tapped into them, others Wesley started. A few of these societies could even trace their history back to the 17th century. As some of these societies grew in size they became a little unwieldy, so they tended to divide into a number of smaller groups, known as bands, which in the early days usually numbered from between five and ten members each. These were the forerunners of the Methodist classes. It was these societies and classes that became the structure and strength of Methodism. Wesley had no time for solitary religion. To him, the Christian life was one of communion and community.

One of these societies was established in Fetter Lane in London, which became a central Methodist meeting place in the early days. True to Wesley's practice, eleven rules were introduced, which each member was expected to live by. They included meeting together weekly for prayer and spiritual support and confessing their sins to one another. New members were accepted on trial for a two month period and if there was no objection to their inclusion they were then admitted into the society.

Though they were Methodists, they belonged to the Church of

England. John Wesley and even more so Charles Wesley thought of themselves as Church of England ministers. Indeed, they had each been ordained to that office. To them Methodism was not to be a body outside that church, it was to be a vigorous part of it.

CHAPTER 6

LAUNCHING OUT IN FAITH

'There never was less religious feeling [in England], either within the Establishment or without, than when Wesley blew his trumpet, and awakened those who slept.' (Robert Southey)

In the middle of June John Wesley went with a few companions to Holland and then for a longer period to Germany. His main aim was to meet with some of the leading Moravians in Hernhuth and learn more from them. He returned to London in the middle of September.

In the closing months of the year Wesley preached in various churches and prisons in and around London, presenting his 'new' Gospel. Some of his listeners responded to it, trusting in Christ. Yet the response from his fellow clergy was not usually favourable and more churches were closed to him.

The year 1739 was to be a significant one for Wesley. On the first day of that year he held a 'love feast' at Fetter Lane with over sixty companions, including his brother, Charles, Benjamin Ingham and George Whitefield, who had recently returned from Georgia. In that meeting 'the power of God came mightily' upon them and 'many cried out for exceeding joy'. Holding a special gathering on the first day or the first Sunday of the year was to become a common practice in Methodist circles.

John Wesley was not the only Church of England minister being banned from preaching in some Anglican churches. George Whitefield suffered it too. Whitefield's ministry in England at this time contained two main thrusts: preaching the word and raising money for an orphan house in Georgia. The latter was one of the reasons he had returned to Britain. Some of the clergy that Whitefield encountered were sympathetic towards helping the orphans but they did not like his preaching. They did not approve of the evangelistic thrust of his message and they found his manner too flamboyant.

Whitefield did not just preach with his voice but with every fibre of his being. He spoke with great energy and when he told a biblical story he acted it out vividly. All this, with the power of the Holy Spirit, made his sermons dynamic and confrontational. His 'listeners' did not just hear the message, they felt it. Under Whitefield people could believe the Gospel or they could reject the Gospel, but it was hard for them to ignore it. His manner of speech was so striking that even single syllables could be compelling. The famous actor David Garrick declared 'I would give a hundred guineas if I could say "Oh" like Mr Whitefield.'

In February Whitefield moved to Bristol in the south-west of England. He was always concerned about those in jail, so on the morning of Saturday the seventeenth he preached in the nearby prison. He was also concerned about the local colliers, who were regarded as godless people, so later that day he went with a companion to nearby Kingswood, where they were most numerous, and began to preach at Hanham Mount. A crowd of over 200 quickly assembled.

Whitefield had now broken the ice! He had dared to preach out of doors, which, even to him, was a little irregular. The following Wednesday afternoon he returned to the field in Kingswood to preach again to the miners. This time he estimated that he had 3,000 listeners. He did so again two days later and this time his hearers were much more numerous. He continued to minister in churches when they were open to him and in the open air when they were not. Crowds repeatedly flocked to hear him.

However, Whitefield was wrestling with a call to go to London. He hesitated to go as he feared that the work at Kingswood would suffer if he did, so he wrote to John Wesley, inviting him to Bristol to take over from him. At first Wesley was reluctant to go. He was busy in London preaching to different societies and was pleased with his progress. Then a second invitation arrived. This time Wesley was much more sympathetic to the request, so he discussed it with his London friends and his brother. They all opposed the visit, believing that he was more needed in London. In fact, 'Charles could scarce bear the mention of it'. However, John eventually decided to accept the invitation. He arrived in Bristol on the last day of March. The next day Whitefield preached in the open air three times.

Wesley, however, now found himself faced with a problem. He was uneasy about the propriety of this open air preaching. Whitefield's actions in this regard seem to have shocked him. As Wesley put it, 'I could scarce reconcile myself at first to this strange way of preaching in the fields; having been all my life (till very lately) so tenacious of every point relating to decency and order, that I should have thought the saving of souls almost a sin, if it had not been done in a church.' He seems to have resolved the issue by preaching later that day *indoors* on Christ's Sermon on the Mount. If it was right for Jesus to preach in the fields, surely it was right for him to do so too.

So Wesley took to the fields. Whitefield had by this time left, but the inhabitants of Kingswood seemed quite pleased with his replacement. Wesley's first outdoor sermon attracted, by his estimate, about 3,000. He preached on the text 'The Spirit of the Lord God is upon me, because the Lord hath anointed me to preach good tidings unto the meek; he hath sent me to bind up the brokenhearted, to proclaim liberty to the captives, and the opening of prison to them that are bound; to proclaim the acceptable year of the Lord.' (Isaiah 61:1-2) John Wesley had found his ministry.

On 21 May, Wesley was preaching in the open air to about 2,000 people on 'Be still and know that I am God.' (Psalm 46:10) Some in the crowd proved anything but still and were certainly not silent. Wesley later recorded that 'One and another and another was struck down to the earth', trembling at the presence of the power of God. Others cried out, 'What must I do to be saved?' By the time he had finished seven people, previously unknown to him, were thanking God for saving them.

That evening Wesley met with a smaller number in a house in Nicholas Street. Soon after he began his address one of his listeners 'groaned' for God's mercy. Wesley continued on. Then another person fell down as if struck. A few moments later a young boy did the same. Standing at the back of the room was a young man named Thomas Maxfield. As Maxfield listened to Wesley he was also overcome and fell to the floor as though dead. But he was very much alive. He soon began to 'roar out' and beat himself against the floor furiously. Six men grabbed him in an effort to quieten him and to stop him hurting himself.

But the matter did not end there. Others from inside the house and more listening from outside began to cry out for God's mercy. The place 'was in an uproar'. Wesley and his helpers prayed for those under conviction of sin. By the time they all parted most had 'found rest to their souls'. Thomas Maxfield was one of them.

Not all those who experienced these outbursts were genuinely experiencing a work of God. One twelve-year-old girl that Charles Wesley interviewed admitted that she had deliberately cried out to attract the preacher's attention. But in other cases it was the Holy Spirit making people aware of their sinfulness and their need of a Saviour.

Wesley's visit to Bristol had also given him an idea. He noticed that Kingswood was swarming with children. They were uneducated, wild and unkempt. So he set a plan in motion to have a school built for them and he began to raise funds for that purpose.

While in the south-west of England, Wesley also preached in Bath, a very fashionable town. While there he had an encounter with Richard 'Beau' Nash. He was the leading figure in that city, a ladies' man and a heavy gambler. Nash accused Wesley to his face of frightening 'people out of their wits' with his preaching.

Wesley asked, 'Sir, did you ever hear me preach?'

'No!'

'How then can you judge of what you have never heard?'

'Sir, by common report.'

'"Common report" is not enough', responded Wesley. 'Is not your name Nash?'

'Yes, Nash is my name.'

'Sir,' said Wesley, 'I dare not judge you by common report.'

***

In 1735 John Wesley missed out on securing the Epworth parish. At that time, wondering what to do next, he asked his Bishop whether his ordination bound him to take on a parish. The Bishop replied, 'It does not seem to me that at your ordination you engaged yourself to undertake the cure of any parish, provided you can as a clergyman better serve God and His Church in your present or some other station.' Some other station! But where would that station be and what would it entail?

From his time in Bristol in 1739 John Wesley developed his philosophy of ministry. He wonderfully described it in a letter: 'I look upon all the world as my parish'. Not that in the strictest sense the whole world became his parish, for from this time he did not move out of the British Isles, except for a brief visit to Holland in 1783. But the point was that he recognised no parish boundaries for his ministry. He began travelling throughout Britain and Ireland preaching the Gospel. He would do it in churches, where it was permitted and practicable, and in fields and on street corners, where it was not. To him there were no restrictions on where he should preach, except for those forced upon him.

Charles Wesley also began to travel around the country preaching in the open air. It is a mistake to think of the younger brother as 'only' a hymn writer. In his early years he was a travelling preacher of passion and power who also attracted large crowds. He was a more emotional preacher than his brother and often concluded his sermons by 'singing an invitation to sinners' to respond to the Gospel. His mother had urged him to make poetry his diversion, never his business, and he certainly had more than one string to his bow. He considered taking on a parish in 1740 and thus end his itinerant ministry, but nothing came of it. So in the 1740s three members of Oxford's Holy Club exercised highly successful travelling ministries: the two Wesley brothers and George Whitefield.

Inevitably, not all approved of what that trio were doing. Local parish ministers often complained about these outsiders muscling in on their territory. In August 1739, the Bishop of Bristol summoned John Wesley to meet him. The Bishop told Wesley, 'You are not commissioned to preach in this diocese. Therefore, I advise you to go hence.' So Wesley left, but only for a time.

John Wesley's usual method of travel on his preaching missions was by horseback, though, especially in his early days, he did sometimes walk. But horse travel in the 18th century was not always safe. Some areas had to be avoided because of highwaymen. Many roads were dangerous, especially in bad weather, so injuries occurred at times to him or his mount, when his horse stumbled or slipped, or led him into trees in the dark.

As far back as 1733 Wesley had had a bad fall when his horse tumbled off a bridge. In Bristol in 1739 his horse fell, casting him to the ground. In 1747, again in Bristol, a cart came quickly down a hill and collided with Wesley's mount. Wesley was tipped over the horse's head and crashed to the ground as the poor beast fell. Both rider and horse recovered to continue the journey, but for a time a rumour circulated that Wesley had been killed in the accident.

Also, England being England, the weather was often bad. Therefore he rode through rain (be it a downpour or drizzle), snow, fog and even at times sunshine. On occasions he became lost. As his brother once colourfully recorded, on one trip 'We lost our way as often as we could'. Yet he travelled throughout the British Isles on horseback for most of the next forty years, then later by carriage, visiting hundreds of cities, towns and villages. He went to so many places, some many times, that by the 1770s his face must have been the most recognisable in Britain. Only the faces of the kings of England, with their heads embossed on the coins, may have been better known.

Wesley's travelling and preaching was also done to a plan. It was not haphazard. He was a methodical man. It was mapped out so that he could do the most possible in the shortest time. Occasionally because of emergencies and divine leading, he would change his plans, but usually he stuck to them. The people in the towns he visited usually knew that he was coming. This was a comfort and an encouragement for his supporters but it meant that his opponents also knew about it, so it gave them time to plot trouble.

***

On Sunday 29 April 1739 George Whitefield preached 'to an exceeding great multitude' in Moorfields, close to the centre of London. Moorfields, as the name suggests, was a vast open expanse, capable of holding many thousands. (It was built over less than 40 years later.) Early that evening he preached at Kennington Common, a place where criminals were hanged, to an estimated 30,000 people. The following Sunday morning Whitefield was back at Moorfields preaching to a crowd of 20,000 and he returned again the next Sunday to speak to 'a prodigious number'. That August, after preaching to great crowds in a variety of places, Whitefield embarked on a ship to return to Georgia.

John Wesley went back to London and took his turn at Moorfields. He arrived, with a handful of companions, at 7 am on a Sunday in the middle of June. A large crowd had already assembled. The little group of Methodists sang a hymn and then Wesley mounted a small platform and faced the crowd. 'He stroked back his hair' and preached on 'Ho, everyone that thirsteth, come ye to the waters.' (Isaiah 55:1)

A rugged stonemason named John Nelson, who came from Birstall in Yorkshire, was amongst the crowd of over 6,000 that day. He said that Wesley 'turned his face to where I stood and I thought fixed his eyes on me. His countenance struck such an awful dread upon me before I heard him speak that it made my heart beat like the pendulum of a clock, and when he did speak I thought his whole discourse was aimed at me.' More importantly, the arrows of the Gospel message were aimed at him and they struck home. Nelson later became one of Wesley's leading preachers in Yorkshire.

In the early evening on the same day Wesley preached at Kennington Common. He spoke from Isaiah 45:22 on 'Look unto me, and be ye saved, all ye ends of the earth' to about 15,000 people.

On Sunday 9 September he returned to Moorfields, where he preached on 'What must I do to be saved?' (Acts 16:30) to about 10,000. That evening he went to Kennington Common again. Amongst his companions this time was his mother, who was not by any means put out by her son's unorthodox activities. She was just one of a reported 20,000 listeners on this occasion.

But not all in these crowds had their minds on the Gospel. Where people gather in large numbers, traders frequently seize the opportunities presented. Often on the fringes of these massive crowds, pedlars set up stalls to cater to the people's more material needs.

If Wesley was not attracting crowds quite as large as Whitefield, he was still drawing vast numbers. Though the claimed figures for both men may have been exaggerated, they still seem to have been preaching to massive crowds. But why did such large numbers attend their preaching?

One practical answer to that is that they were both great speakers, though by common consent Whitefield was the better of the two. They also had a vital message and they presented it in a challenging way. But there was also a spiritual dynamic that was outside the control of either of these two men. The Spirit of God was moving powerfully in London at that time and He made the 'foolishness of preaching' attractive and fruitful. As will be seen, in the future Wesley did not always draw such large numbers as he did in 1739, but there were later times when he again did so.

Wesley hit the nail on the head when he said, 'the devil does not love field preaching'. How could he? There were too many being converted to Christ through it for him to favour it. But, perhaps oddly, Wesley said, 'Neither do I love it. I love a commodious room, a soft cushion, a handsome pulpit.' He went on 'But where is my zeal, if I do not trample all these underfoot in order to save one more soul?' So again and again he went out into the fields to preach.

CHAPTER 7

CONFLICT

Wesley made a frequent practice of visiting prisoners in jail, especially those who were under the death sentence. On 12 February 1740 he visited Gwillam Snowde, who was in a prison in London and due to be executed the next day. His crime, ironically, had been against Methodism. He had stolen £30 from a charity that was raising money to aid Wesley's school at Kingswood, but he now seemed genuinely repentant. The next day Wesley heard that the date for the execution had been put back six weeks. Eventually, Snowde was reprieved and transported instead. Whether Wesley had intervened in some way to achieve this, if that was possible, is unclear.

A little later, Wesley made repeated visits to a soldier on death row. Wesley presented the Gospel to him and he became a Christian. However, it made no difference to his earthly fate. At the end of March he was executed.

John Wesley returned to Bristol several times in 1740. On his arrival there in March he found his listeners somewhat more subdued than in the previous year, but God was still working in the hearts of many of them. After a short visit to Wales he returned to Bristol again on 12 April.

He did not stay there long this time. He heard about a dispute in the Fetter Lane Society, principally about Holy Communion and the nature of faith, so he rushed to London to deal with it. The problems were being caused by a recently arrived Moravian named Molther. Herr Molther was saying that if one did not have assurance of faith, then one was not saved. He also argued that the means of grace, such as church attendance, prayer, reading the Scriptures and taking communion were useless for the unconverted, which now included, according to him, those without assurance of salvation. He believed that the only way to faith in Christ was 'to be still'.

After Wesley's visit to Hernhuth in 1738 he had expressed some doubts about certain Moravian beliefs in a letter that he never sent. He loved the Moravians and admired them, but he was not blind to their faults. Now Moravian-inspired problems had arisen in the Methodist society in London.

Charles Wesley, while in London, vigorously countered Molther's arguments, but to no avail. The society was in chaos.

Charles needed the support of the more forceful John to deal with the problem. So when the older brother arrived in London, they both went to visit Molther and debated the issue. But Molther would not budge. They visited him again without success. They also visited various troubled members of the society and found them confused and downcast. John Wesley preached and counselled but made little headway.

Duty called John Wesley elsewhere but he returned in June and again in July. Matters at Fetter Lane were no better on either occasion. Eventually the society split in two over the disputed issues, those siding with Molther stayed at Fetter Lane, those remaining loyal to the Wesleys moved to the Foundery, an old disused arsenal. Though the Wesleys had been greatly helped by the Moravians, from this time a gap existed between them.

The following year John Wesley had a meeting with Count Zinzendorf, a leading Moravian, to see if they could heal the rift, but no good came out of it. Later the Count stated publicly that the Wesleys would 'soon run their heads against the wall'. Wesley responded, 'We will not if we can help it.' Yet Wesley could still say that next to the best in the Church of England, the Moravians, were 'in the main ... the best Christians in the world', even allowing for their mistakes.

In 1743 the number of Methodists in London had increased to nearly 2,000. The Moravians in that city numbered about 70.

***

On one of his visits to Bristol in 1740 Wesley preached what became known as his 'Free Grace Sermon'. His text was 'He that spared not his Son, but delivered him up for us all, how shall he not with him also freely give us all things.' (Romans 8:32)

'How freely does God love the world?' he asked his hearers. He answered the question for them:

> While we were yet sinners 'Christ died for the ungodly'. While we were 'dead in sin', God 'spared not his own Son' but delivered him up for us all. The grace or love of God, whence cometh our salvation, is free in all, and free for all.

> First, it is free in all to whom it is given. It does not depend on any power or merit in man; no, not in any degree, neither in whole nor in part. It does not in anywise depend either on the good works or righteousness of the receiver; not on anything he has done, or anything he is. It does not depend on his endeavours. It does not depend on his good tempers or good desires, or good purposes and intentions. Thus is God's grace free in all.

> But is it free for all, as well as in all?

He then proceeded to make a deliberate attack on the Calvinistic understanding of predestination. He made it clear that he believed that 'predestination is not a doctrine of God', at least in its Calvinistic form.

He then proceeded to give a number of reasons why he rejected it.

He closed with 'O hear ye this, ye that forget God. Ye cannot charge your death upon him. Repent and turn from all your transgressions. "Turn ye, turn ye from your evil ways; for why will you die, O house of Israel?"'

This sermon caused a little controversy when it was first preached, but not more. Probably few of his listeners detected the controversial aspects of it. However, later that year Wesley published it is as a pamphlet. That did cause trouble. And division! He also sent the booklet to friends in America, which widened the dispute. Whitefield published a response and the battle was on.

The division was caused by the disagreement between Wesley and Whitefield over predestination and election to salvation and issues related to those doctrines. Wesley was an Arminian, Whitefield a Calvinist.

Ironically, Wesley accepted the idea of God's election of certain people to salvation. But his understanding of it was different from that held by the Calvinists. To the Calvinist, God elected some to salvation simply by His sovereign choice. There was nothing in those so elected, now or in the future, that caused His choice. To Wesley and other traditional Arminians God elected to salvation those He foreknew would believe in Christ.

The disagreement was over more than that, but the different understanding of election and God's foreknowledge were the crucial issues. Wesley had come to this conclusion about foreknowledge as far back as 1725. His mother had held the same view, and there is some evidence that he learnt it from her.

Though the doctrinal gap between Wesley and Whitefield was not as wide as some suppose, it did cause a major rift between them. For some time feelings ran high, particularly from their respective supporters. It is said that at one stage, early in the conflict, Whitefield went as far as regarding the Wesleys as preaching a different Gospel from him, and he certainly spoke against both Wesleys at times. Yet after the early ructions, Wesley and Whitefield returned to a position where each had deep respect and admiration for the other. However, from this time they rarely worked together in mission.

John Wesley became the undisputed leader of the Methodists, who were Arminian in doctrine. George Whitefield, who did not have leadership ambitions and travelled to America too often to effectively lead a major religious body in Britain, nonetheless became the major figure in Calvinistic Methodism. Charles Wesley sided with his brother.

It is noteworthy that when John Wesley later published his *44 Sermons* and *53 Sermons*, which were intended as doctrinal standards for his preachers, the Free Grace sermon did not appear in either. What this says about his later beliefs may be debated. However, it can be argued that Wesley, ever the Arminian, had moved a little closer to Calvinism. Certainly in August 1745 he said that true Christianity, in other words his form of Arminianism, was 'within a hair's breadth' of Calvinism. The two theologies were close, identical in some respects, but different. His sermon on free grace, however, must be seen as a little further from Calvinism than 'a hair's breadth'.

CHAPTER 8

METHODISM

John Wesley's aim was to spread scriptural holiness throughout the land. That is, his intention was not just to win people to Christ, but also to see that they lived holy lives that glorified God.

As Methodism grew, Wesley had to find an effective method of organisation, which encouraged that. With his discipline and skills it was always going to be an efficiently organised movement. But the method had to allow for the fact that it was essentially a part of the Church of England. To John Wesley, and even more to his brother, Charles, Methodism was not a separate church. The Wesleys were ordained Church of England clergymen and they had not left that church. Though many in the Church of England disapproved of their methods, the fact remained that they had neither resigned nor been dismissed. The movement that they led, therefore, was also part of the Anglican Church. They did, however, later build separate meeting houses and chapels for their people to use for worship.

As the work expanded Wesley grouped his converts in societies, and they were societies, not churches. Early in 1742 the London society had grown to about 1,100 widely scattered members. This was clearly unworkable, so he divided it. Societies were further divided into smaller groups called classes, each with a designated class leader, who exercised pastoral oversight. Each class usually met weekly for mutual support and the confession of sin.

At first Wesley concentrated on London, the counties that surround it and Bristol. He then extended his ministry further in the south-west into Cornwall, Wales and north into Yorkshire. By 1746 the number of Methodist societies had increased so much in Britain that Wesley grouped them into seven circuits. That is, all the societies in one area were linked together to form an associated group called a circuit. The size of these circuits varied depending on the region, mainly whether it was a country district or a city or major town. Some of these circuits, particularly in the early years, covered a wide area, though others were much smaller. The number of circuits also increased as time progressed. By 1753 there were twelve of them.

Each circuit held business meetings quarterly, at which the leaders of that society met to discuss the circuit's affairs. These meetings became known as 'Quarterly Meetings'.

To serve the societies Wesley introduced two kinds of preachers. First, there were circuit ministers, fulltime preachers, some who were ordained and some who were not. A circuit minister had to travel his circuit, usually on horseback, preaching the word and supporting the various societies in his circuit. Secondly, there were local preachers. These were all laymen, usually with other fulltime work. As their name suggests, they usually only served a local area.

Perhaps the first Methodist lay preacher was John Cennick, who also wrote a number of hymns and the grace 'Be present at our table, Lord'. He later left Wesley after a dispute on predestination and joined the Moravians. But probably the most prominent lay preacher in the early days was Thomas Maxfield, who had been converted so dramatically through John Wesley in Bristol in 1739.

Maxfield had begun preaching the Gospel at the Foundery in London, the new Methodist meeting place in London, while John Wesley was away on one of his trips. At that stage, Wesley firmly believed that only ordained ministers should be allowed to preach, but Maxfield was a layman. This deeply disturbed Wesley, so he hurried back to London.

At that time Susanna Wesley, approaching the end of her life, was living in the Foundery. She cautioned her son not to act hastily, telling him 'I charge you before God, beware what you do; for Thomas Maxfield is as much called to preach the Gospel as ever you were.' Wesley took his mother's advice and heard Maxfield preach. Wesley was so impressed he raised no objection to his continuing to do so. By the end of 1740 Wesley had sent out at least 20 lay preachers.

Though Wesley permitted laymen to preach, he did not allow these lay preachers, whether circuit ministers or not, to give the sacraments. In other words, he did not allow them to baptise or officiate at the Lord's Supper. As there were few ordained men in the Methodist ranks, it was normal practice for Methodist leaders to encourage their people to attend their local Anglican church for baptism and Holy Communion.

From 1744 the governing body in Methodism was the conference. At the first conference John Wesley met with his brother and four other Anglican clergymen and four laymen. They discussed a variety of doctrinal, organisational and disciplinary matters. The conference eventually met annually in the middle of the year and was held in a number of major towns and cities, including London, Bristol and Leeds.

It is clear that John Wesley dominated these conferences. What the conference discussed was usually what John Wesley wanted discussed. What the conference decided was usually what John Wesley decided. Even his brother, Charles, was well in his shade.

At one conference John was speaking for a long time and Charles cried out, 'Stop that man from speaking. Let us attend to business.'

But John continued on, which caused Charles to interrupt again. 'Unless he stops, I'll leave the conference.'

John responded, 'Reach him his hat.'

Towards the end of July 1742 John Wesley returned to London. He found his mother 'on the borders of eternity'. She died peacefully on the evening of 23 July. On 1 August John conducted her funeral service before an 'innumerable company of people'. She was buried at London's Bunhill Fields, near the Foundery, close to the graves of John Bunyan and Isaac Watts.

CHAPTER 9

WESLEY ENCOUNTERS THE MOBS

No one engages in the kind of work Wesley undertook without opposition, and sometimes opposition of a violent kind. John Wesley certainly experienced this, but in a remarkable way he most often remained serene and unharmed amidst it.

At the end of March 1740 Wesley was preaching in Bristol, when 'Some or other of the children of Belial' tried to shout him down. On the first day of the following month the opposition became worse, 'all the host of the aliens' had joined together to disrupt his preaching, with people 'shouting, cursing and swearing, and ready to swallow the ground in fierceness and rage.' It was a dangerous situation.

The Mayor sent an official to order the troublemakers to disperse, but they took no notice. He next sent the Chief-Constable, but the mob threatened him. One man was never going to quieten the rabble. Finally, the Mayor sent a number of officers with instructions to arrest the ringleaders, which they did.

The next day the arrested men appeared before the Mayor. When given opportunity to speak they laid all the blame on Wesley, accusing him of a variety of 'crimes'. But the Mayor was not deceived. He told them 'What Mr Wesley is, is nothing to you. I will keep the peace. I will have no rioting in this city.'

But not all officials in the various British towns were as kind to Wesley and the Methodists. In some they ignored the troubles or sided with the rioters.

One Sunday evening that September, while returning to his home in London, a large 'mob' gathered around Wesley and hemmed him in. Strangely, he later recorded, 'I rejoiced and blessed God, knowing this was the time I had long been looking for.' One suspects that not many other people would have seen this encounter in quite that light. But he was grateful for the appearance of this informal, if somewhat frightening, congregation and he preached to them on 'righteousness and judgement to come'. At first, few in the crowd could hear what he said because of the great noise that they were making, but gradually they quietened and listened to him. When he had finished and prepared to part from them, they all showed him 'much love'. We might wonder at the quality of that love, but that is how he reported it.

That same month William Seward, an associate of George White-field and Charles Wesley, was on a preaching tour in Wales with How-ell Harris, the great Welsh preacher. Someone in the crowd threw a stone, which hit Seward in the eye. The missile caused him to become blind in that eye and a few weeks later he died. Whether or not the blow from the stone caused his death is not known.

Yet another member of the Seward family, Henry, was anti-Method-ist. He strongly opposed Charles Wesley. He called the younger Wesley 'rogue, rascal, villain and pickpocket', and even threatened him with two pistols. Fortunately, Henry Seward decided to place the guns back in his pockets, but then proceeded to grab Charles by the nose, which he held and pulled until Mrs Seward came to Wesley's rescue. The Method-ist decided not to retaliate and instead sang 'Praise God from whom all blessings flow', presumably with a nasally twang.

On 25 January 1742 John Wesley was preaching in a house in Lon-don, with people crowded inside and out. Some of those outside, though, had not come to listen. They began to push and jostle the people that they could reach and threw large stones on the roof of the house. This caused tiles to come cascading down upon those inside. Wesley addressed the aggressors directly, warning them that they would be taken before the magistrate if they persisted, but they took no notice. They continued to yell out abuse and throw rocks onto the roof.

But Wesley had plenty of supporters inside the house. He sent a few of his more robust helpers outside, to grab the ringleader and bring him inside. The man reluctantly entered the home swearing at the top of his voice, with the mob shouting out his name. But suddenly he quietened, for, Wesley said, 'God had struck him to the heart.' After that the situation calmed.

***

John Wesley did not believe in wasting time. Time spent on horseback was not just useful for travelling, but also for reading or talking to people that he met. His general practice was to mount his horse, set it travelling in the right direction and then read as the horse made its way, changing direction or stopping when necessary.

He had a particular liking for the ancient classics, both Christian and secular. On one occasion, travelling in the north of England, he read Xenophon's *Memorabilia* of Socrates, and later recorded that he was 'amazed at his want of judgement', though whether it was Xenophon or Socrates who was lacking is not entirely clear. On another ride in the north a few years later he read Homer's *Iliad*, which he enjoyed, in spite of its 'pagan prejudices'. It is clear that Wesley did not just read these books, he thought seriously and critically about them.

In the evening of Friday 28 May 1742, still engrossed in Socrates, he arrived in Newcastle-upon-Tyne, on his first trip to the north of England. His attention was soon diverted, however, by the sights he witnessed on a short walk through the town. 'I was surprised,' he later recorded in his journal. 'So much drunkenness, cursing and swearing, even from the mouths of little children, do I never remember to have seen and heard before,' and in the places he had visited he had seen and heard much. 'Surely this place,' he wrote, 'is ripe for Him who "came not to call the righteous, but sinners to repentance."'

On Sunday morning he went with a friend, John Taylor, to an area, which, in Wesley's judgement, was 'the poorest and most contempt-ible' part of the city. They found a good spot and began singing the hundredth Psalm. Within moments people started to gather. By the time Wesley began to preach 500 or so had assembled. Wesley preached from 'He was wounded for our transgressions, he was bruised for our iniquities. The chastisement of our peace was upon him, and by his stripes we are healed.' (Isaiah 53:5)

The people listened intently, some with mouths opened in astonish-ment. A minister preaching in the streets, and preaching to them, was something new. When Wesley concluded the crowd had increased to over 1,000. After his sermon Wesley introduced himself and invited the people to come back at 5 pm, when he intended to preach again.

Wesley kept his promise and returned a little before five. This time the situation was different. The crowd was much more numerous. The hill near where he had stood in the morning 'was covered from the top to the bottom'. Wesley said that he had never seen 'so large a number of people together, either in Moorfields or at Kennington Common.' As, on one occasion, he had estimated a crowd of 20,000 at Kenning-ton Common, the Newcastle crowd must have been a vast number, even allowing for some exaggeration.

He preached on 'I will heal their backsliding, I will love them free-ly' (Hosea 14:4), but doubted that his voice, powerful though it was, could be heard by all of that great assembly. When he had finished, hundreds gathered around him and hemmed him in and were in danger of crushing him, but there was no violence.

On 5 June he visited Epworth, his old home town, and stayed at the inn. There was not much of a welcome. Only three or four old acquaintances, including an old family servant, visited him there.

The next day, a Sunday, he went to the church early and offered to help the curate in the day's service. That afternoon the church was unusually full, as the news spread that Wesley would be preaching. But the curate had rejected Wesley's offer and preached against the kind of religion he believed the Wesleys advocated.

As the people were leaving the church, John Taylor shouted out that Wesley would preach in the church grounds at 6 pm. When Wesley arrived to keep that appointment, a large assembly had gathered and he stood on his father's tombstone and preached on 'The kingdom of heaven is not meat and drink; but righteousness and peace, and joy in the Holy Ghost.' (Romans 14:17) The people listened intently, though there was not much positive response, nor was there any trouble.

For the next few days he preached in neighbouring towns and villages and returned to Epworth on Friday. There he preached about Ezekiel's vision of the dry bones. This time the response was different. He recorded, 'great indeed was the shaking' amongst the crowd and 'lamentation and great mourning were heard'. On Saturday he spoke on 'the righteousness of the Law and the righteousness of faith'. While he was speaking 'several' of his listeners 'dropped down as dead'. Others cried out so loudly that they almost drowned out Wesley's voice. 'But many of these soon lifted up their heads with joy and broke out into thanksgiving.'

Wesley reflected in his journal that his father and mother had ministered at Epworth for many years and he for a few, though with little result. Now the harvest had come.

***

Yet danger always loomed. In some areas anyone who aligned with the Methodist cause was likely to be harassed or attacked. Wesley had visited the western midland county of Staffordshire in January 1743. His visit had been fruitful. Many joined the Methodists while he was there and more did so after he had left.

But all was not peaceful. A group of local troublemakers began to stir up the people against them. It was made worse when one of Wesley's preachers made some untactful remarks about the local clergy. The vicar of Wednesbury responded in kind and opposition to Methodism rose to a most dangerous level.

In the middle of June, while Wesley was in London, the wrath of the mob descended upon the Wednesbury Methodists. For six days there was rioting. Methodist preachers were attacked, some were held under water until nearly dead, others were daubed in paint, and it is probable that some women were raped. When Methodists met together the mob would descend on them, throwing eggs, rotten fruit and whatever else came to hand. The magistrates did nothing, or at least nothing effective.

Wesley was shocked and went to support his Staffordshire flock. He arrived in Wednesbury on 22 June. He only stayed for two days, but visited the local councillor, who advised that Wesley's people prosecute their attackers. Wesley conveyed the message and moved on.

There was a lull for a while, but in October, John Wesley rode again into Wednesbury. Soon after his arrival he preached on 'Jesus Christ, the same yesterday, and today, and for ever' (Hebrews 13:8) and afterwards retired to the home of a friend. That afternoon a crowd gathered around the house. The Christians prayed. The crowd dispersed.

Later a much larger and more aggressive mob collected outside the house. 'Bring out the minister!' dozens of voices demanded. 'Bring out the minister!'

Even the brave John Wesley thought going out to meet them unwise. But with a stroke of genius, he invited the ringleader into the house. Wesley calmed him down and invited two more of the leaders in. These two entered in an angry mood, but after encountering Wesley's calm manner, they cooled down.

By this time Wesley felt that he dared venture outside, so he did. He called for a chair, which was quickly brought to him. He stood on it and addressed the hundreds now assembled. 'What do you want with me?' he cried out.

'We want you to go with us to the Justice. Let him decide what to do with you.'

'I am willing to do that,' said Wesley. The mob quietened. Wesley stole the moment and told them a little about himself and why he was in their town.

'So when shall we go to the Justice? Tonight or tomorrow morning?' he asked.

'Tonight! Tonight!' came the immediate response.

So Wesley went to see the local Justice of the Peace, followed by 100 or more of his antagonists and three or four of his supporters. Others from the mob had now lost interest and gone home. By the time they had arrived at the house of the Justice night had fallen. They knocked on the door, though the noise they were making was enough to make their presence known. A servant opened the door and told them that the Justice, Mr Lane, was in bed. The mob insisted on seeing him, but the servant had by this time now received reinforcements in the person of Mr Lane's son. He told them, 'Go home and be quick and quiet about it.'

Realising that they were going to get nowhere with Mr Lane, they formed another plan. They decided to go to see the Justice in Walsall. Once more when they arrived the Justice was in bed and refused to see them.

By this time it was all becoming a bore and many began the walk home. About fifty, however, agreed to escort Wesley back to his lodgings. They did not get far before a much bigger mob from Walsall descended upon them. A woman, a leading figure in the Wednesbury group, seems to have thought that the best form of defence was attack, and immediately began to fight the men from Walsall. However, she and her companions were soon overcome and the out-numbered crowd from Wednesbury quickly scattered, nursing their wounds.

John Wesley was now in the hands of the angry men from Walsall.

They took hold of him and marched him into the centre of their town. He tried to escape, but one of the antagonists brought him to an abrupt halt by grabbing his hair and dragging him back. They continued on. All the while he spoke to them in an effort to calm them, but to little effect. As they marched on, Wesley noticed that the door of a nearby shop was open. He made a dash for it, but the owner barred his way, afraid of what might happen if he let him in.

Wesley decided to make a stand outside the shop and attempted to speak to the crowd again. 'Listen to me', he called out. 'What evil have I done that you should treat me so? What have I done to hurt you?'

'Kill 'im! Death to the Methodist! Death to the Methodist!' The mob's mood was getting blacker by the minute. Wesley's powerful voice was drowned in the din.

But Wesley prayed.

Suddenly a large man ran towards him. For a moment the preacher thought the worst. But instead of an act of aggression the man spoke to him. 'Sir, I will spend my life for you,' he said. 'Follow me, and not one soul shall touch a hair of your head.' Three more men joined Wesley's rescuer and they formed a protective ring around him.

Then the shopkeeper, who also happened to be the local magistrate, with a sudden burst of courage cried out to the crowd, 'Shame on you! Shame on you all! Let the poor man go.'

A nearby butcher then entered the fray and knocked down some of the leading troublemakers. Wesley's new found friends made the most of the moment and half-shepherded, half-carried the preacher to safety. Wesley survived with nothing worse than torn clothing and a few minor cuts and bruises.

Afterwards Wesley reflected on the providence of God and how the Lord had seen him through such a dangerous string of experiences. He also wrote in his journal that throughout that dangerous time he had the 'same presence of mind, as if I had been sitting in my own study.' For a moment, though, he had feared that they might throw him into the river. His main concern, it seems, was that if that had happened 'it would spoil the papers' in his pocket. He was confident that he could have swum to the other side.

Among the Staffordshire Methodists were Joshua Constable and his wife, who lived in Darlaston. At the end of January 1744 Mrs Constable was travelling to neighbouring Wednesbury when she was attacked by a band of thugs. They threw her to the ground, held her down and seemed ready to rape her, but for some reason they changed their plan and beat her up instead. One of the offenders was taken before the courts but was released.

This judicial action, or inaction, seemed to make matters worse. A week after that attack the rabble ransacked the Constables' home, but fortunately when they were out. The mob wrecked what they did not steal. Afterwards the house was in such a mess that the family was unable to live there, and their neighbours were reluctant to offer hospitality to them and their children for fear of the mob. In fact, the troublemakers smashed the windows and inflicted other damage on some nearby houses as a warning against such kindness. The Constable family was homeless. And this in winter!

In the following days threats were also made to some of the Methodists in Wednesbury. However, those threatened made it clear that they would defend themselves and their property if attacked. The aggressors backed off for a while. But after a few days delay they carried out their threats and attacked every Methodist home they could identify. They smashed windows wrecked furniture, stole goods. One poor woman who was asleep when the attack started was tipped out of her bed, which was then smashed to pieces around her.

Though these attacks were carried out by the rougher elements in the community, they were encouraged by some of the local gentry, the land owners and employers. They warned that if any of their workers invited more Methodist preachers into their town, they would lose their jobs.

Then Charles Wesley arrived in the area. But the expected explosion did not occur immediately.

The rioters next spread their attacks to nearby Aldridge. These attacks followed the same pattern with homes being damaged and property stolen. The destroyers then made their way back through Walsall with the loot. But some of the leading men in that town had gathered a group together, and they confronted the troublemakers. They confiscated the stolen property and sent word back to Aldridge that the owners could come and collect it.

In spite of this fierce persecution, or perhaps because of it, the County of Staffordshire was to become a Methodist stronghold.

CHAPTER 10

MORE TROUBLE

The year 1744 did not begin well. On 10 January Wesley visited the Methodist society in Bristol and the next day 'began examining' it individual by individual. He was not pleased with what he discovered. 'The plague was begun', he recorded in his journal. But this was no physical plague, but a spiritual one. Many of those he interviewed cried out 'Faith! Faith! Believe! Believe!' but showed no fruits of faith, no holiness and no good works.

In Wesley's thinking, there was hardly a greater heresy than 'faith' that did not lead to holiness and good deeds. He was with Paul in believing that we are saved by grace through faith in Jesus Christ, not by good works. He had long ago learned from bitter experience that no one can be saved by human effort. But he was also with James, that 'faith without works is dead'. (James 2:20) True faith in Christ would always lead to good deeds. Those deeds did not save but they were the inevitable outworking of saving faith.

He set about eradicating the plague of 'faith' that does not lead to good works and spent several days teaching them 'a more thorough understanding of the truth as it is in Jesus'. By the time he left Bristol, he believed that he had been successful.

However, this experience was not easily forgotten. He moved on to Bath and seems to have been concerned that the plague may have spread to there, for he preached from James 2:14, 'can faith save him?'

As he spoke one 'gentlewoman', overcome with emotion, 'broke out into strong cries and tears'.

But good news soon came from an unexpected corner: France. In February he received a letter from John Haime, a British soldier on duty on the continent. Haime reported that he had begun a Methodist society in his regiment the previous year and that this had now grown to a dozen. Later in the year Haime told Wesley that his society had about 200 members and his preaching was at times listened to by many more.

But long life is not guaranteed in the army. Several of the society's leaders, but not Haime, were killed in battle, and Methodism in that regiment struggled for a while. When going into battle Haime told his comrades, 'If I fall this day, I shall rest in the everlasting arms of Christ.' In one battle he was nearly killed when his horse was shot from under him, but he was later able to return to England, leave the army and join the ranks of Methodist preachers, at times travelling with Wesley.

In the early months of the 1744 rumours also abounded that the French would soon invade England, which brought fears of a Catholic takeover. The rumours had some foundation, as a little later Louis XV of France assembled a fleet threatening to invade the south-east of England to support Bonnie Prince Charlie.

This fear of invasion influenced Wesley's preaching and other aspects of Methodist observance at this time. For a few days in January he preached on 'Watch ye therefore, and pray always, that ye may be accounted worthy to escape all these things that shall come to pass, and to stand before the Son of Man.' (Luke 21:36) 'Cry mightily unto God ... turn every one from his evil way' (Jonah 3:8) and 'Our God whom we serve is able to deliver us from the burning fiery furnace, and he will deliver us out of thine hand, O king. But if not, be it known unto thee ... that we will not serve thy gods.' (Daniel 3:17-18)

Friday 17 January had been designated as a national day of prayer and fasting because of the feared invasion. Wesley met with the society in London that afternoon, and in spite of the demands of work 'many' came together. Some days later a storm scattered the French ships and the invasion never took place, though a year later Prince Charles did arrive in Scotland.

Persecution against Methodists continued on into 1744 in a number of places, partly caused by the belief that Methodists were Catholics under another name. Wesley became so concerned about this and the lack of action from the relevant authorities that he penned a letter intended for King George II. He respectfully drew the king's attention to the real nature of Methodism and assured the king of the loyalty, support and prayers of the Methodist people. He then changed his mind and decided not to send it. Instead he published it in his journal.

A couple of weeks later Wesley was called before the Justices of the Peace in Surrey. The charge was that he was encouraging loyalty to the Pope. This he strongly denied, swore the oath in support of King George and signed 'the declaration against popery'. He was then allowed to go.

This shows that there was a lot of confusion about what Wesley and his followers believed. He was known to be a minister in the Church of England but seemed to be founding his own sect. He argued that his beliefs and practices were in agreement with the English church, but people detected differences from what he said and did and the lives and beliefs of other Anglican clergy. One major problem was that these differences appeared against the backdrop of a possible French (Catholic) invasion of England. Methodism's differences made people nervous and the rumour mill only made that worse.

Wesley was a fine and experienced horseman. But even the most able riders have mishaps. In March that year, on yet another trip to Bristol, his horse fell and he was dumped awkwardly on the ground. Wesley rose to his feet covered in mud from head to foot but was unhurt. He checked his horse, cleaned himself up a bit, remounted and continued on his way. Two days later he arrived in Kingswood, preached there in the early afternoon, and then went on to Bristol where he preached again in the evening.

There were also attacks on Methodists in Cornwall in the south-west of England. In July 1743 Charles Wesley visited St Ives. He had not been well. The local clergy did not welcome his visit and they encouraged the people to oppose him.

One morning Charles set himself up in the market place and he and a few supporters began singing the hundredth Psalm. But many in the crowd that had gathered had not come to listen or pray. Their aim was disruption. Some beat drums and others shouted to drown out the singing. When the time came for Charles to preach he stood for a while in preparation but the noise was so great it was clearly pointless. He called out to the main troublemakers, offering to speak with them privately to discuss their grievances, but they were not in the mood for a quiet discussion.

Suddenly a group of them charged forward and grabbed the preacher. But Charles, whose 'soul was calm and fearless' eluded them. Then the Mayor arrived on the scene. He was more intent on justice than some of his fellows in Staffordshire.

'Stop this rioting', he cried. His voice cracked as he shouted his message. 'Leave that man alone and go to your homes. If this continues, you'll face the courts.'

The noise subsided. Those who had taken hold of Charles Wesley, took their hands off him, and sheepishly looked at the Mayor. Wesley turned to him, and thanked him.

'Go to your homes, I say', the Mayor said forcefully once more.

Gradually, reluctantly, the crowd began to disperse. It was not long before nearly all of them had vanished, taking their drums with them. A few stayed behind to speak to Wesley.

A few days later Charles was preaching in a meeting house when the mob attacked. It burst into the building, threatening murder and striking those within range. Charles pleaded with them to desist, but the attack was only repelled when the aggressors forgot what they had come for and began attacking each other.

Brother John arrived in St Ives at the end of that August, where Charles had previously carried out a successful work. John first met with the members of the local Methodist Society, who by this time numbered over a hundred, most of whom, in his judgement, were genuinely converted.

The opposition that soon assembled, however, misidentified John. As he walked through the streets they sang,

Charles Wesley has come to town,
To try if he can pull the churches down.

Not that either of the Wesleys were interested in pulling 'the churches down', but that is how many often saw them: as enemies of the church.

On this trip to St Ives, John Wesley also visited some of the surrounding villages, preaching to crowds of anything from a hundred to a thousand. These congregations, which often consisted mainly of tin miners, were more attentive and supportive than many he encountered.

Back in St Ives in the middle of September Wesley met with his people at the local Methodist meeting place. The service went peaceably enough until some ruffians burst in, 'roaring and striking those who stood in their way'. Wesley quickly identified the leader of the rabble, moved into the middle of the furore and grabbed hold of the man. Wesley then led him to the desk, separating him from his companions. In the scuffle one of the rioters hit Wesley on the head, but the preacher was not seriously hurt. Wesley then reasoned with the mob's now isolated leader. 'Sir, we mean you no harm,' he told him. 'You need fear nothing from us. We preach salvation through Jesus Christ to you and to all men.' The man soon quietened down, as did his followers.

On this visit to the south-west, Wesley took opportunity to see the ruggedly violent Land's End. He was deeply impressed. He described it as 'an awful sight', with the sea boiling 'as a pot'. Later he described the craggy rocks at Land's End as 'torn by the sea', which made them 'like great heaps of ruins'.

The following year a mob from St Ives destroyed the local Methodist meeting place. This occurred just after a triumph by the British navy. Wesley satirically observed that the crowd pulled down the building 'for joy that Admiral Matthews had beaten the Spaniards'. He added, 'Such is the method of Cornish thanksgiving'.

On another visit to Cornwall in July 1745, John Wesley arrived in Falmouth. One afternoon he visited a sick woman named Kitty. While in her home he became aware of a disturbance outside the house. A large and noisy mob was gathering and their focus was on John Wesley. Kitty and her daughter went to the door to try to calm them, but the noise grew louder and the mood blacker.

'Bring out the Methodist! Bring out the Methodist!' they cried.

The two women retreated and hastily locked the door and entered one of the rooms. But the mob surged forward and burst through the front door. The inner door protected the three from immediate harm, but it was clear that that would not last long. Wesley and the two women prayed briefly but loud banging on that door interrupted them.

'Get into the closet, Mr Wesley. Get into the closet,' Kitty said.

'No, my dear, it is best for me to stand where I am.'

Suddenly the door was forced open and Wesley was face to face with the ringleaders of the mob. Other rioters were pushing from behind to try to get into the room. There was noise, there was anger.

Wesley took the initiative. 'Here I am', he said. 'What have any of you to say to me?'

The mob's rush was suddenly brought to a halt.

'To which of you have I done any wrong? To you?' Wesley pointed straight at one man. 'Or you? Or you?' He pointed to others. 'Let me into the street and I will address the people.'

So saying, he pushed his way out of the house and took his stand in the street. With the command of a Roman General, he addressed the quietening throng. 'Neighbours, Countrymen! Do you desire to hear me speak?'

For a moment there was silence, which was strange enough on this day. Then up went the cry, 'Yes! Yes! Let him speak.'

So Wesley addressed them, introducing himself and stating his purpose. They listened in silence.

While he was speaking, a Reverend Thomas and an alderman arrived on the scene, plus two other leading figures of the town. When Wesley had finished they escorted him to safety, though, in truth, the danger was past.

Wesley later made the point that he deliberately had not worn his hat when he ventured outdoors on that occasion so that the crowd could see his face clearly. He knew from past experience that the calm demeanour evident in his face had a soothing effect on others. It was a remarkable feature of a remarkable man.

When Wesley arrived in the harbour city of Plymouth in the far south of England late in the evening of 26 June 1747 the place was in an uproar. There had been an anti-Methodist riot the previous day, and when Wesley arrived, a mob still congregated outside the home of a leading local Methodist.

Wesley and his travelling companions rode slowly towards the mob. The crowd shouted aggressively but parted to allow the travellers through. The visitors entered the home but the rabble continued their watch for another hour, making a half-hearted attempt to break into the house, before they tired of their sport and departed.

Wesley spent much of the next day speaking to the various members of the local society. There was no sign of any troublemakers. At 6 pm Wesley and a few associates gathered in the open air. They began by singing a hymn. As they sang, the crowd gathered.

Before the hymn finished the sound of drums could be heard and it was getting louder each moment. Then on to the scene burst some soldiers and drummers followed by the mob. The hymn came to an inglorious conclusion amidst the sound of the pounding drums and shouting people.

John Wesley liked to continue according to plan when that was possible. He thought of getting up on a stand to preach but as the hubbub continued he soon realised that that was pointless. There was just too much noise. So he enacted plan B. He pushed his way into the midst of the rabble and walked up to a large man who appeared to be the leader.

Wesley held out his hand to shake that of his adversary. The antagonist was stunned. For a moment he did nothing and said nothing. Then slowly his right hand moved up and forward and clasped Wesley's hand.

'Sir,' he said to Wesley, 'I will see you safe home. No man shall touch you.'

Then the man shouted to the crowd, 'Stand off! Get back! I will knock the first man down who touches him.'

The crowd parted. Wesley and his new found friend walked through the gap. Shouts of abuse were still directed at Wesley but his protector, with a fierce look and roars of anger, silenced the aggressors. They walked on to the house of Wesley's host where the preacher shook hands again with his guard and they then parted company. Wesley and his hosts had a peaceful night.

Early the following morning, a Sunday, Wesley preached on the nearby common to a 'well-behaved and earnest congregation'. A few hours later he moved to another location and proclaimed to a larger but still attentive crowd 'Seek ye the Lord while he may be found'. (Isaiah 55:6)

Wesley's method of dealing with trouble and confronting troublemakers was remarkable. It never should be doubted that there were occasions when he was in serious danger and even a few times when he was injured. But he could have been severely beaten or killed on numerous occasions. Was God protecting him? Yes, no doubt He was, as He did with the Apostle Paul centuries before. But there seem to have been other factors as well. Wesley's demeanour: his calmness, his confidence, his friendliness, perhaps even the kindliness of his face, often disarmed even the most aggressive of opponents. A group of soldiers to whom he spoke on one occasion declared there was 'something superhuman' about him. His appearance, his manner seemed to overcome opposition. He thus usually escaped serious harm.

Riding and preaching, riding and preaching, in good weather and bad, so his life continued. And the weather that Spring was terrible. When it was not snowing, it was raining, and heavily, with strong, biting winds. Yet he continued on and still people ventured out to listen to him.

A mob in Plymouth had also confronted Charles Wesley the previous year. He refused to yield to its demands for him to leave the city and deliberately stayed longer than he originally intended. He felt that if the opposition was that fierce, then the devil must be alarmed by his presence, so further attacks on his principality were necessary.

CHAPTER 11

TWO NEW HELPERS

Opposition there was, but converts too. One of them was Peter Jaco (1729-81). Jaco was from Cornwall, born in Newlyn, near Penzance. He was brought up to honour God but in his teens he lived only for pleasure. But the more he sought pleasure, the more miserable he felt.

Early in the evening of 12 July 1747, John Wesley visited Newlyn, taking his stand on the sandy beach. An immense and noisy multitude gathered to greet him. He began by praying and the people soon quietened. But the silence was not for long. A group of troublemakers arrived from Penzance and began pushing through the crowd, swearing as they went. They eventually reached the front of the assembly and began to menace Wesley.

The tall and imposing Peter Jaco was in the crowd that day with some of his mates. They saw the threat, moved forward and surrounded Wesley to protect him. The aggressors took one look at the sizeable Jaco and his companions and decided to retreat. Wesley did what he always did in such circumstances: he seized his opportunity and preached the Gospel.

Soon after this, Jaco, though still unconverted, joined the local Methodist society. Wesley's preaching had made an impact upon him. For some months Jaco agonised through a period under deep conviction of sin. One afternoon he was walking to church when the thought 'Jesus Christ died for the vilest sinner' went through his mind. Then suddenly realisation came to him: 'Then I am the wretch for whom He died'. That moment, as he later said, he became 'a new creation'.

A couple of years later he began to exhort in the meetings of his local society. A year or so after that Wesley returned and persuaded him to work with a number of Cornish societies. In 1754 the Methodist Conference appointed him as a circuit minister in the Manchester Circuit, which covered a large part of the north of England. His ministry there was greatly blessed by God.

By the late 1770s he was obese and his mobility was restricted, which caused him to retire from the itinerant ministry. John Wesley put it this way, 'Peter Jaco would willingly travel. But how? Can you help us to a horse that will carry him and his wife? What a pity we could not procure a camel or an elephant.' But in spite of this Jaco was 'steadfast in all the storms of life'.

Towards the end of August 1748 Wesley visited Haworth in Yorkshire. (Haworth was later to become famous as the home of the Brontë sisters.) At that time the imposing William Grimshaw was the Anglican minister there. Grimshaw was originally antagonistic towards the Methodists, but by this time he was much more sympathetic. He was a man that one could not ignore and he preached with great power.

Grimshaw had been born in Lancashire in the north of England in 1708, and as a young man, had attended Cambridge University. He entered the ministry unconverted but later endured a prolonged period under conviction of sin. This did not end until he had a vision of Christ pleading to God on his behalf. He begged for forgiveness and trusted Christ. As he later recalled, at that time 'what light and comfort did I enjoy in my own soul, and what a taste of the pardoning love of God.' He then became a genuine minister of the Gospel.

When he first became the minister in Haworth in 1742 he was largely unknown. His ministry initially was just to the people of Haworth and a few neighbouring villages, but as time progressed, his fearless and evangelistic preaching attracted people from a wide area.

He was dedicated and energetic. He often preached 15 times or more a week, which was a punishing schedule. He also showed great compassion for the less fortunate in his parish, especially in visiting the elderly and sick. Early in his time in Haworth he discovered that some of the poor in that locality were reluctant to attend church because they lacked suitable clothes to wear. So he set aside Sunday evenings for services especially for them, so that they could hear the Gospel without feeling embarrassed.

John Wesley had great admiration for him. He said of Grimshaw, 'A few such as him would make a nation tremble. He carries fire wherever he goes.'

The day after his arrival in Haworth that August Wesley preached at 5 am in the Haworth Church, and even at that hour it was nearly full and by the time the service concluded it was packed. The following day Wesley and Grimshaw rode on to Roughlee to preach there. On their way they were warned by sympathisers on a number of occasions not to go on because a mob was assembling, intent on doing them harm.

However, they arrived safely and Wesley began to preach at half an hour after midday. At first it was all peaceful. But when Wesley was halfway through his sermon, 'the mob came pouring down the hill like a torrent'. They were obviously not intending to listen to a sermon as some of the men were armed with clubs. Wesley saw the danger, broke off preaching and, as was his practice, spoke to the leader of the rabble, who claimed to be a Deputy-Constable.

'I order you to cease this preaching,' said the deputy, his face red with anger. 'Come with me immediately to the Chief-Constable's house. He'll know what to do with you.'

'I will gladly do so. Lead the way,' responded Wesley.

So the deputy led the way and Wesley followed. But before they had walked 10 metres one of the mob smashed his fist into Wesley's face. Then a stick came flying through the air and hit him on the head. Wesley stopped and tried to reason with the deputy to make him calm his followers. While he was doing so, another man began to wave his club threateningly at the Methodist leader.

The situation calmed down slightly and they again began walking to meet the Chief-Constable. A drummer had placed himself at the head of the parade, which only attracted more to join the motley throng. When they reached their destination, Wesley, Grimshaw and two supporters were brought before the Chief-Constable. He was not sympathetic.

'Mr Wesley,' he said, 'I want you to promise never to go to Roughlee again. Nor should you send any other Methodists.'

There was silence for a moment as Wesley thought out his response. Then he stated boldly, 'I would rather cut off my hand than make such a promise. Neither I nor my preachers can promise that. We go where we are called to go: into all the world.'

The Chief-Constable and those with him would not accept that. They insisted that he should not go back to that town. They argued on and on, with the constable lecturing the preacher on 'justice and law'. Wesley hardly got a word in. Occasionally he asked to be allowed to leave but his requests were ignored. After a while the aggressors fell silent. This gave Wesley time to clear his thoughts and think about what his reply should be. 'I will not preach at Roughlee today', he said. 'That is the best I can do.'

The Chief-Constable considered his position. 'Right! And make sure you don't. You can go.' With that, he went out the door and addressed the mob. 'Now quieten down and go home all of you. I will deal with this matter, not you. No rioting! No more trouble!'

The mob did quieten, but no one moved away. They waited to see what would happen next. The Chief-Constable went back into his house and told Wesley, 'You may go. And don't cause any more trouble.'

Wesley went out one door, Grimshaw and the others went out another. Suddenly the previously silent mob became a roaring mass. Threats and oaths filled the air and a shower of stones flew towards Wesley. The atmosphere was thick with aggression. One man knocked Wesley to the ground. He struggled to his feet, but because of the crush of bodies was unable to move in the direction he wished and he was forced back inside the house.

Grimshaw and his companions fared worse. They were knocked about, thrown to the ground and covered in muck and dirt. There seemed to be no escape.

There were some other Methodists on the fringes of the crowd watching with horror but they were too few in number and too far away to help. Some in the mob identified these witnesses and turned their wrath upon them also. However, they were in a better position to run away than Wesley and his companions, and so they did, but few escaped. Some were beaten, while others were knocked down and dragged along by their hair. One was given the choice of jumping more than three metres into the river or being pushed into it. He chose to jump.

The authorities took no notice. They had had their say. To them the matter was over.

When the mob had tired of its sport, the Methodists limped home battered and bruised.

In later years John Wesley was thinking of naming Grimshaw as his successor as leader of Methodism. However, the dedicated Grimshaw died in 1763 of a fever that he caught while visiting a sick parishioner.

In the middle of the 18th century Methodist preachers were commonly bombarded with eggs and rotten vegetables. Threats to them were common, violence not unusual. Some were half-drowned, others beaten nearly to death. But in a strange way, all this furthered the Methodist cause. The preachers became objects of sympathy rather than hate. People learned that they could trust them and began to support and follow them.

As the years rolled on, Wesley and his followers experienced less opposition. The people they ministered to became more favourably disposed towards them and the authorities also became more sympathetic.

CHAPTER 12

IRELAND

'No one is fit to be a preacher (in Ireland) who is not ready to die any moment' (an early Methodist preacher), recorded in *The Dictionary of Methodism.*

England and Wales had been mainly Protestant countries since the Reformation. Yet the reception the Wesleys and Methodism received in those lands was often hot rather than warm. Their brand of Christianity was frequently not welcomed by the majority. It was opposed by the mobs and often by the authorities and by the Anglican Church.

Ireland was traditionally and mainly Catholic, with about 80 percent of the population subscribing to that faith. The main Protestant enclaves were in the north (Ulster), where a substantial number belonged to either the Church of Ireland (which later joined with the Church of England) or the Presbyterian Church. The Church of Ireland also had a firm base in Dublin, though it was in the minority. Other denominations were tiny.

In the summer of 1747 Wesley decided to pay Ireland a visit. This was one place Wesley could not get to on horseback. He, like everyone else, had to catch a boat to get there. Aware of the large Catholic majority, Wesley must have wondered how he and his Methodism would be received in that land.

Wesley first arrived in Dublin on 9 August that year with fellow preacher, Billy Tucker. Upon arrival, Wesley sent a message of introduction to St Mary's Church and the curate of that church invited him to preach that day. Wesley did, but ministered to what he called as 'senseless a congregation as I ever saw'.

George Whitefield had visited Dublin some years before, so a Methodist society already existed there. Wesley called the society together and at 5 am the next day they all met in a large, crowded room. He preached on 'Repent, and believe the Gospel' (Mark 1:15). He proclaimed, 'Awake thou that sleepest. Know thyself to be a sinner, and what manner of sinner thou art. Know the corruption of thy inmost nature, whereby thou art gone from original righteousness. Know that thou art corrupted in every power, in every faculty of thy soul; that thou art totally corrupt in every one of these.' Wesley was ever uncompromising in laying bare the sinfulness of the human heart.

But human hearts could be healed through faith in Christ and repentance. 'Believe this,' he urged his listeners, 'by faith thou attainest the promise. "God pardoneth and absolveth all that truly repent and believe his holy gospel". And what is to believe? It is not just a bare assent to the truth of the Bible or the articles of our creed. The devils believe this and yet they are devils still. But it is, over and above this, a sure trust in the mercy of God, through Christ Jesus. It is confidence in a pardoning God.'

His subject on this occasion suggests that he suspected that many of his hearers, though part of a Methodist society, were not converted. He found this congregation much more responsive than the one on the previous day. They listened intently and they 'all seemed to taste the good word'.

Later that morning Wesley returned to St Mary's to speak to the curate. The clergyman was friendly but uncooperative.

'Mr Wesley, I appreciated your help yesterday, but I'm afraid I can no longer allow you to participate in our work here. I don't approve of your methods.'

'My methods! What specifically don't you approve?'

The curate hesitated for a moment. He was clearly embarrassed. 'Field preaching for one', he began. 'The Gospel should be preached in our churches not in the open air. Then I've also heard you allow unordained men to preach. That's clearly against the laws of our church. The Archbishop of Dublin has told us we are not to cooperate with you.'

'The Archbishop? Then I must meet with him and explain why we are doing these things.' So Wesley went to the top and paid the Archbishop a visit. The Archbishop may have seen him coming, for by the time Wesley arrived he was not at home.

It was Wesley's practice to interview the members of each Methodist society to enquire into their spiritual condition. This was a demanding and time-consuming task, which, in the end, he had to give up when Methodist societies and the people they contained became too many. But on this occasion he was able to speak with many members of the Dublin society, but whether it was all 280 of them must be doubted. He noted that the vast majority were not native born Irish men and women, but had come from England or Scotland. Yet he found them 'in general of a more teachable spirit than men and women in most parts of England.'

As early as the second day of his visit to Dublin, Wesley recognised the need for a leading Methodist to stay there for a prolonged period. However, he could not. Other duties called, so he planned to move on, but not wanting to leave the struggling Irish societies orphaned, he sent a message to his brother to come and replace him. So John Wesley left Ireland a mere two weeks after his arrival but he was to visit that land many more times.

Two weeks later, brother Charles arrived in Dublin. He found the situation amongst the Methodist society chaotic. Persecution had arisen, which discouraged many from meeting together. Also, few were willing to allow their homes to be used for Methodist meetings, for fear of the mob.

Yet Charles did not blame them for their caution, for he also experienced the danger. As he walked the streets people cursed and threatened him. Even members of the Church of Ireland verbally abused him.

Charles battled on in Ireland well into 1748. He widened his ministry into the area surrounding Dublin and established a firm base for future Methodist work. However, numerical growth was small.

On 24 February 1748 John Wesley arrived at Holyhead in northern Wales to catch a vessel to return to Ireland to join his brother. After four days of frustration, waiting for one to sail, he penned a poem:

There are, unless my memory fail,
Five causes why we should not sail:
The fog is thick; the wind is high;
It rains; or may do by-and-by
Or – any other reason why.

In the end he gave up and stayed in Wales for a further week, ministering in a number of towns in Anglesey. Knowing no Welsh, he usually had to preach through an interpreter, yet the people responded well.

But Ireland still called, so it was back to Holyhead to catch a boat. The vessel eventually left for Ireland in the early hours of 8 March. Once on board he soon went to sleep but was woken by a fierce storm. In contrast to the response to the storm he experienced on his way to America, he seems to have taken it in his stride and hardly referred to it in his journal.

Upon arriving in Ireland, he hired a horse and rode to Dublin. A few days after his arrival, his brother returned to England.

Wesley usually had a good relationship with the horses that carried him the thousands of kilometres throughout the British Isles. He did not have a romanticised view of them but knew how important they were to his work. In his later instructions to his preachers, he even included a clause on the treatment of horses. 'Be merciful to your beast,' he said. 'Not only ride moderately but see with your own eyes that your horse be rubbed, fed and bedded.'

However, for anyone that spends a great deal of time on the backs of horses, there are going to be mishaps. One afternoon early that April, Wesley mounted his horse, which immediately began to snort and run backwards. Wesley tried to gain control but the mount leapt from side to side, crashed into a gate and threw him out of the saddle to the ground. Wesley, shaken but unhurt, rose to his feet and sought to calm the animal. It responded placidly.

Early on this visit Wesley and some companions encountered a drunken man, who was 'very zealous for the Church'. He told the Methodists, 'No gown, no crown.' Wesley shared a few biblical truths with him and when they left him he was 'full of good resolutions'. However, it seems that these resolutions only 'held several days'.

For the most part, the welcome John Wesley received from the Irish was polite, even kind, though on one occasion a large section of his audience kept mocking him, after which a friar tried to shout him down, by crying out, 'You lie! You lie!' In fact, many Catholic priests had forbidden their people from attending his meetings. However, the people still went to listen to him, which caused the priests to attend Wesley's preaching to try to lead their people away.

Wesley had a negative view of Roman Catholicism but he was not a bigot. He believed that Catholics were 'heretics', and 'enemies to us, and to our church and nation.' But he urged his people to treat them well.

Early one Sunday morning in Athlone he preached in the open to over 300 people. When he had concluded, he went to visit a sick woman who lived just outside the town. As he walked he was aware of a commotion behind him. He looked back and saw a substantial part of the congregation following him. These people did not want him to leave them. When he left the house after ministering to the woman, the crowd was still waiting. He found a suitable spot, asked everyone to kneel down and then prayed. He then led them in singing a Psalm and spoke to them briefly from the Scriptures.

Sometimes when he preached, many of his listeners were in tears but Wesley reflected that in most cases no lasting work was done. It appeared that for the majority, the sorrow was superficial. On one occasion he preached 'the terrors of the Lord', but his listeners did 'not appear to digest any part of it'.

His health was poor for part of this visit. He had a fever that lasted several days, and on occasions his voice was affected. Yet he still travelled and he still preached, though on one ride he found it difficult to stay mounted. He left Ireland to return to Wales in the middle of May.

He returned to Ireland in April 1749. When he arrived in Dublin, he interviewed the members of the society and found that in the year it had risen from 400 to 449. This was a reasonable increase, especially when one considers that Wesley was strict on deleting from the roll any who did not behave in a Christian manner. His aim was not numerical increases but making true disciples of Christ.

CHAPTER 13

THE ROMANCE

'I fell, while love's envenomed dart
Thrilled through my nerves and tore my heart.'
(John Wesley, 'Reflections on Past Providences').

James Hutton, John Wesley's publisher, told Count Zinzendorf, a leading Moravian, 'The Wesleys are a snare to young women. All fall in love with them.' While Hutton does not appear to have mentioned it, there was also the danger that young women could be a snare to the Wesley brothers.

At the beginning of August 1748 John Wesley was grappling with a bad and persistent headache, which was sometimes accompanied by bouts of vomiting. Yet it did not often stop him preaching, nor did it not stop him travelling. On the twelfth of that month he arrived in Newcastle-upon-Tyne.

His headache persisted but in Newcastle he found a nurse, an attractive and intelligent, 32 year old widow named Grace Murray. Grace was a native of Newcastle but had moved to London when she was 18. Two years later she married a Scottish sailor, Alexander Murray, and gave birth to a child. The baby died. This caused the bereaved woman to look for answers. She found at least some of them in Methodism. In 1742 her husband died at sea, so she returned to Newcastle. In that city and beyond she became recognised as a dedicated Methodist. She lovingly ministered to about 100 people in a number of Methodist classes.

That same year John Wesley commissioned the building of a home for orphans in Newcastle. The orphan house was, in fact, a multi-purpose building. It housed orphans but it also functioned as a Methodist meeting place and when either of the Wesleys was in Newcastle he stayed there. It also served as a rest home for battle-worn Methodist preachers.

The following year he appointed Grace Murray as the home's housekeeper. Wesley had a high opinion of her. He described her as being 'nicely frugal', though not mean, she made 'everything go as far as it can go', had 'much commonsense', was 'indefatigably patient' and did everything quickly, but 'without hurry'. As far as John Wesley was concerned she was the ideal woman for the job. Indeed, he began to think of her as the ideal woman.

He later wrote a poem, in which he said of her,

In early dawn of life, serene,
Mild, sweet and tender was her mood;
Her pleasing form spoke all within
Soft and compassionately good;
Listening to every wretch's care
Mingling with each her friendly tear.

In Newcastle's orphan home in August 1748 Wesley benefit-ted from Grace Murray's ministrations for three days. Grace Murray cooled Wesley's pounding head, but raised the temperature of his heart. Wesley was not the first, nor the last, to fall in love with his nurse. 'If ever I marry,' he told her, 'I think you will be the person.'

She replied, 'This is too great a blessing for me; I can't tell how to believe it. This is all I could ask for under heaven.' In short, that meant yes, providing Wesley's 'if' could be overcome. While Wesley's words to her were a kind of proposal, it was the sort that raised as much doubt as confidence.

Yet this was a significant step for Wesley. Both he and his brother Charles had more or less resigned themselves to celibacy in the cause of Christ. When a minister was madly travelling around the country preaching, taking a wife along presented difficulties, and if children came, then those difficulties were greatly multiplied. It would generally mean that if the itinerancy continued, there would be frequent periods of separation from his family, some of them for weeks or even months. Each of the Wesleys had also agreed not to marry without the consent of the other brother. That John Wesley's previous romantic encounters had not ended well only added further uncertainty.

John Wesley had no intention of changing his lifestyle. For the next few weeks he travelled around the north of England in the company of some fellow preachers, with Grace Murray also in the party. It was as if he was testing her to see if she could take the rigours of a campaign.

As it turned out this campaign turned nasty and resulted in an attack by yet another mob. The preachers and their accompanying supporters were treated severely. It would seem that Grace was still with them, so she must have suffered along with the rest. The mob beat them with sticks, threw stones at them and covered them in mud and dirt. They even pulled some along by their hair. At one stage, Wesley was beaten to the ground. What made matters more shameful was that the leader of the rabble claimed to be the local Deputy-Constable. The next day Wesley wrote a stern letter of complaint to the Chief-Constable.

Grace Murray had also nursed other Methodist workers. One of them was John Bennet. Bennet was one of Wesley's first preachers. He worked in the north of England, itinerating through Lancashire, Cheshire, Yorkshire and Derbyshire. He had fallen ill in 1746 and Grace Murray had nursed him back to health. Like Wesley after him, he had felt attracted to Mrs Murray.

Bennet was also in the party with Wesley and Murray in the attack just mentioned. After that incident, the group split, Wesley and some of the others moved on, but Grace Murray and John Bennet stayed behind. Wesley preached in the north for a while and then went south, preaching in the Midlands, London, and as far west as Cornwall. He was away from Grace for a number of months.

However, Bennet's close proximity to Mrs Murray revived his feelings for her. He fell in love with her. But the road ahead was far from clear. He was aware of Wesley's liking for Grace but did not know whether the Methodist leader viewed her as just a friend or whether he was contemplating marrying her.

So he asked her, 'Is there anything between you and John Wesley?'
'No!'
Bennet felt his spirits lift. 'Would you consent to marry me?'
Grace Murray was in a quandary. Certainly she had no firm commitment with Wesley, but she had given him the impression that if he proposed, she would say yes. But would he propose? At that moment Wesley was many kilometres to the south with lots of other things on his mind. Did he ever think of her, she wondered. Probably yes, but did that make it any more likely that he would propose to her?
'Yes, Mr Bennet, I will marry you, but only if Mr Wesley approves.'
Both Bennet and Murray wrote to Wesley detailing this surprising new development. Presumably at least one of these letters asked for Wesley's approval. Wesley was stunned. This was an event that he had, rather naïvely, not anticipated. Whether Wesley's approval was necessary or not for the marriage, it was not immediately forthcoming.

That the Wesley brothers had agreed to consult each other about possible marriage plans both complicated and slowed down their courtships. Yet John's hesitation seems to have had as much to do with his inner turmoil as his brother's lack of support.

While John Wesley dithered, his brother, Charles, did marry. On

Saturday 8 April 1749 John Wesley recorded in his diary, 'I married my brother and Sarah Gwynne. It was a solemn day, such as became the dignity of a Christian marriage.' And that was that.

At about that time John Wesley sent Grace a letter inviting her to accompany him and Billy Tucker on a lengthy tour of Wales and Ireland. He wanted her to organise female classes and help with the wider work amongst women. It would seem likely that he also hoped that this might renew her affection for him. She accepted the offer and assisted Wesley in countless ways, both personally and in ministry.

They returned to England, visiting Bristol and London and they then travelled north to Newcastle. They ended up in Epworth, Wesley's home ground. Then John Bennet turned up. This caused the love tangle to twist further. Wesley argued with Bennet. Grace expressed her love for Wesley, but wondered whether she ought to marry Bennet. Wesley thought she might be better off if she did marry his rival. At one point she told Wesley, 'I love you a thousand times better than I ever loved John Bennet. But I'm afraid if I don't marry him, he'll go mad.' Love or duty! Wesley did not know how to respond to that. It only increased his confusion and his mental agony.

The matter was finally settled by one outside the trio: Charles Wesley. Strangely, the recently married Charles had been for some time trying to persuade his older brother not to marry. He objected to Grace herself, regarding her as inferior, but he was also concerned that marriage would slow down his brother's work. This objection added further to John's confusion.

After further indecision from all the parties, on 3 October Grace Murray married John Bennet. Charles Wesley conducted the ceremony.

Caught briefly in the midst of this turmoil was George Whitefield, who had appeared on the scene again. It became his mournful duty to convey the sad news to John Wesley that Grace Murray had married John

Bennet. Whitefield did 'all that was in his power to comfort' his old friend, but Wesley found little relief from his sadness. In a letter written just afterwards, Wesley said, 'The fatal, irrevocable stroke was struck on Tuesday. Yesterday I saw my friend (that was), and him to whom she is sacrificed. I believe you never saw such a scene.' He also recorded the Scripture, 'The Lord gave, and the Lord hath taken away: blessed be the name of the Lord!' (Job 1:21) It is little wonder that he also prayed,

O Lord ... why did Thou the blessing send?
Or why thus snatch away my friend?

John Wesley blamed both his brother and Bennet for his unfortunate loss, Charles for his 'impetuosity' and Bennet for acting 'against the will of God'. The relationship between the two Wesleys not surprisingly soured for a while; that between the two Johns completely ruptured a little later, with Bennet going to join the Calvinists, taking some of the societies that he pastored with him.

Amidst all this turmoil and heartache Wesley, remarkably, continued his ministry, travelling from one town to the next and then to the next. He preached in town squares and fields and ministered devotedly to the Methodist societies, which were growing in number and size. His journal of this period shows little sign of the emotional upheaval he was going through. It was almost as if he was living in two different worlds at once, the ministerial and the personal.

CHAPTER 14

FURTHER MINISTRY. FURTHER STRIFE

'We are forbid to go to Newgate [Prison], for fear of making them wicked; and to Bedlam [mental asylum], for fear of driving them mad!' (John Wesley's Journal, 22 Feb. 1750).

In August 1748 Wesley visited Bolton in the northern county of Lancashire. His reception was hot. One Sunday morning he accepted an invitation to preach in a nearby Anglican church and afterwards, as many could not get into the crowded building, he preached again in the churchyard. The outdoors crowd was well behaved. He even commented that it behaved better than some congregations in church.

Early that afternoon he went to Bromley Cross, a part of Bolton. He stood at the top of some steps and prepared to preach. An enormous crowd gathered, but many were more interested in having fun at the preacher's expense than listening to him. In Wesley's own phrase, they were 'utterly wild'. Some were shouting and screaming at each other and at Wesley, while others were fighting.

The crowd seemed to be in a continual state of movement, with troublemakers pushing and jostling. As Wesley warmed to his task, some climbed the steps and threw Wesley down them. He rose to his feet, mounted his makeshift pulpit again, only once more to be grabbed and thrown down the stairs. But Wesley refused to give way. He went up the stairs again and continued preaching. Again they tried to throw him down but a rain of stones aimed at Wesley from another section of the crowd was not well directed. One man, who had been 'bawling' in Wesley's ear, was hit on the cheek by a stone. Another was hit on the forehead. A third stretched out his hand to grab Wesley and a stone smashed into his fingers.

The aggressors at the top of the steps decided that it was not a safe place to be, so quickly descended the stairs and joined the crowd. Wesley continued preaching and gradually the crowd quietened down.

The following October Wesley seems to have sufficiently forgiven John Bennet to accept an invitation from him to preach in Rochdale, another Lancashire town. (This was remarkable on Wesley's part, as it was about two weeks after Bennet had married Grace Murray and Wesley's sense of loss was still deep. He was able to push personal feelings aside for the sake of the Gospel.)

It was Wesley's first visit to Rochdale but its people appear to have known that he was coming, for as he entered the town the streets were lined on both sides with people raging against him. Wesley looked at the angry mob, turned to his companions and said, 'The Apostle Paul "fought with wild beasts at Ephesus" and it looks as though we are in danger of doing the same in Rochdale. Preaching in the fields is too dangerous here. Is there a place indoors we can use that affords us some protection?'

Instantly one of his supporters directed him to a house with a large, upper room. The noisy crowd followed and gathered outside the building. Wesley then spoke to the people through an open window, on 'Let the wicked forsake his way and the unrighteous man his thoughts.' (Isaiah 55:7) The crowd, for the most part, listened in silence.

Wesley and his companions next rode on to Bolton. They were given another hot welcome. The evangelists soon discovered that 'the lions in Rochdale were lambs in comparison with those at Bolton'. As Wesley and his fellow preachers rode to where he was to spend the night, the crowd followed behind them, shouting threats and abuse. When the preachers had entered their host's house, the crowd outside increased dramatically until it stretched from one end of the street to the other.

The noise continued, even increased in volume for a while, but then subsided to a low murmur. 'Was the danger over?' they wondered.

Wesley's host thought so. 'I'll go outside and see whether it's safe for you to preach in the street.'

Wesley grabbed the man's arm. 'Are you sure that's wise?' he asked. 'They are still there.'

'We have to try something.' So saying the brave man opened the door cautiously and slowly stepped out. Immediately, he was set upon by some of the roughs, thrown to the ground and rolled in the mud. He managed to scramble away from them, made a dash for the house and his friends pulled him indoors.

But being inside the house did not guarantee safety, as a stone came through a window. The rioters then began to ring a bell, presumably as a method of calling more to their cause. Wesley was upstairs when the mob broke through the front door. They grabbed John Bennet, who proceeded to tell them forcefully about 'the terrors of the Lord'. Another preacher took a more gentle approach. But neither preacher met with much success.

When Wesley came down the stairs, he noticed that the lower rooms all seemed filled with these uninvited guests, intent on making trouble. He went into the midst of them and called for a chair. One was given him. He stood on it and began to speak. As he addressed them, his 'heart was filled with love', his 'eyes with tears' and his 'mouth with arguments'. At his words, the mob soon ceased to rage and began to listen to him. He later recorded, 'They were amazed; they were ashamed. They were melted down and devoured every word I said.'

At five the next morning he preached to all who could crowd into the house. A few hours later he walked to a nearby meadow and arrived not only unmolested, but welcomed by the gathering crowd. The aggression had now turned to acceptance, the abuse to praise. The lions had indeed, become lambs.

One man deeply touched through Wesley's preaching on this visit was a local barber, one of the most 'eminent drunkards' in Bolton. He later told Wesley that when he heard him preach, God 'struck me to the heart'. The man later prayed that God would give him power to give up the drink. God answered and his desire to drink soon disappeared. Yet still he was not converted. A few months later he felt himself still destined for hell, but God ministered to him in his desperation. It was then that he trusted Christ.

Soon after this visit to Bolton, Wesley visited the Cheshire village of Alpraham. He stood under a pear tree, a site previously used by another Methodist preacher, John Nelson, and proclaimed 'Seek ye the Lord while he may be found'. (Isaiah 55:6) The next day he counselled a number of people concerned about their spiritual condition. Wesley noted that they were not 'publicans and sinners', but rather were like him in his Oxford days, trying to get right with God by good deeds. They had believed that they did not need to repent; now they had suddenly found out that they did.

When Wesley returned to Bolton in April 1753 he found the Methodist society there in a healthy state. The membership had doubled in less than a year and they had 'increased in grace' as much as in number.

Though Wesley could be brave in facing danger, he was not without a sense of caution. On one occasion when he was directed to a yard as a suitable place for preaching, he soon decided against it. The perimeter of the yard was covered in stones, which he deemed useful projectiles for troublemakers.

Wesley made another trip to Ireland early in April 1750. The voyage over was less than pleasant. That was not particularly because of the weather, though it was stormy, rather it was because of 'another storm' that

Wesley met below decks. This storm was human. On board was a notorious man, noted for his loud-mouthed vulgarity. He accosted Wesley with a string of obscenities and blasphemies. Wesley seems to have adopted the policy of not casting 'pearls before swine' and retreated into his cabin.

The weather was bad enough for them to have to return to Holyhead, where the passengers were boarded in an inn. The ruffian then became worse rather than better. He raged and roared, struck the landlord and kicked the landlord's wife.

'I want to see the parson', he shouted at the landlord. 'Bring me the parson.' But it was not spiritual comfort he was after, but trouble.

The landlord rescued Wesley by putting him in a separate room and locking the door. The man broke down a couple of doors in his search for Wesley and then climbed on a chair to get a better view. However, as Wesley observed, he was not 'made for climbing', so he slipped and fell to the floor with a great crash.

Then the landlord's daughter stepped in with a useful solution. She tipped a bucket of water over him, though even that did not silence him. The landlord, who was used to dealing with troublemakers, then locked him in another room and did not let him out until he promised to behave.

Days later Wesley boarded another vessel and arrived in Ireland. He began in Dublin and then travelled through various towns, before arriving in the city of Cork on 19 May. At eight the next morning he preached at Hammond's Marsh to a large and attentive crowd. There was a hint of trouble on the fringes of the gathering but nothing untoward took place.

Early that afternoon Wesley heard that the Mayor was going to refuse to allow him to preach that evening. Wesley thought it best to negotiate rather than run into avoidable strife, so he sent two local Methodists, Messrs Skelton and Jones, to the Mayor to check on the situation.

Skelton asked the Mayor whether it would be in order for Wesley to preach at Hammond's Marsh that evening.

'I'll have no mobbing', said the Mayor.

'But sir, there was none this morning.'

'Oh, yes there was. Aren't there enough churches and meeting houses for you that you have to meet in public places? I will have no more mobs and riots.'

'But', said Skelton, 'there was no mob or a riot this morning. It was all peaceful.'

The Mayor became angry. 'I'll have no more preaching in public places', he said. 'If Mr Wesley attempts to preach again, I'm ready for him.'

That evening Wesley preached in a small meeting house. In spite of this, the Mayor still decided to oppose him. He organised his forces, a group of drummers, whom he instructed to march on the house in which Wesley was ministering. Inside the house Wesley preached, outside the drummers tried to make sure he was not heard. This inevitably attracted a crowd, which soon exhibited the nature of a mob. Inside Wesley spoke, outside the rabble shouted and screamed, accompanied by the still pounding drums.

When Wesley had finished his sermon and emerged from the meeting place, the crowd surged forward and surrounded him, waving sticks and throwing stones The situation was dangerous, not only for Wesley, but for those who followed him into the open. Noticing one of the local officials nearby, Wesley shouted to him, 'Keep order, man. Keep order. You have the authority.' But the man made no attempt to do so.

Wesley decided to take a bold approach that had worked so often in the past. He looked in the eyes of those closest to him and walked forward. Strangely, the aggressors parted and Wesley walked through the midst of them. As he approached Dant's Bridge he came face to face with another mob, shouting 'Here's to Romanism! Down with the Protestants!' Wesley once more looked directly at those nearest to him and this mob also opened up before him and he walked through unmolested.

Some of his fellow Methodists were not so fortunate. Mr Jones was thrown to the ground and rolled in the dirt, and only escaped from his tormentors with difficulty. The mob then burst into the meeting house and wrecked it.

The next afternoon Wesley left Cork to travel to nearby Brandon, followed by a howling mob. At one spot on his route they even burnt an effigy of him. The next day he reappeared at Hammond's Marsh. Once more the drummers marched in and the crowd gathered again and once more became threatening.

Wesley sent for the Mayor. He responded to Wesley's call and arrived with a troop of soldiers. He addressed the crowd, saying 'Lads, I bid you go home.' He then said that again, and again. Not a soul moved. The Mayor then looked about him and said complacently, 'Now I have done.'

With that, the Mayor and the soldiers departed, but the mob did not. It converged upon the nearby home of a Methodist and wrecked it. The following day the rabble was still patrolling the streets with no one to control it. But during the next day or two the mob became smaller and smaller and finally dispersed. The troublemakers seem to have tired of their trouble.

It is clear that in this instance the Mayor's conduct stirred up the crowds. Without his action and inaction, Wesley's visit would probably have been greeted with little disturbance. But the town's leaders, particularly the Mayor, clearly encouraged the locals to threaten and harass Wesley and his supporters.

Wesley was well aware of this. He wrote a letter of protest to the Mayor, which closed:

I fear God and honour the King. I earnestly desire to be at peace with all men. I have not willingly given any offence, either to the Magistrates, the Clergy, or any of the inhabitants of the city of Cork; neither do I desire anything of them, but to be treated (I will not say as a Clergyman, a Gentleman, or a Christian, but) with such justice and humanity as are due to a Jew, a Turk or a Pagan.

Wesley did not expect favourable treatment. He just wished that people, especially those in positions of authority, would treat him and his fellow Methodists in a civilised way.

CHAPTER 15

MARRIAGE

In April 1749 John Wesley had conducted the wedding ceremony for his brother Charles and Sarah (Sally) Gwynne, the daughter of a magistrate. From that time Charles gradually withdrew from the itinerant ministry. Early in October that year Grace Murray, the woman John Wesley adored, had been snatched away from him.

But towards the end of 1750 and early the next year his thoughts were again turning to marriage. Once more a widow was in focus: Mrs Mary (Molly) Vazeille. She was from a Huguenot family. The Huguenots were a Christian group that had been savagely persecuted in France during the previous century. Many of them had left France to escape that persecution and settled in England. Wesley was generally on good terms with them and a number of them became Methodists.

Mary's husband had died, leaving her with four children. She was, by this time, 41 years of age. Wesley was 47.

Wesley consulted with various friends about this course of action, but not his brother. He must have felt unable to trust Charles on this matter. At least two of John's friends, the Rev Vincent Perronet and Ebenezer Blackwell, a banker, seem to have encouraged him to marry. It is even possible that one of them suggested that he marry Mrs Vazeille.

On 2 February Wesley recorded in his journal that he was now 'clearly convinced that [he] ought to marry'. He also stated that 'For many years I remained single, because I believed I could be more useful in a single, than in a married state.' This attitude must have received some severe shocks during his interest in Grace Murray and probably contributed to his hesitancy. But he had now come to believe that he 'might be more useful' married.

His view here sounds well thought out and logical, but not very romantic. It is probably true to say that his relationship with Molly Vazeille was never particularly romantic, whereas his earlier association with Grace had been.

When Charles Wesley heard about his brother's proposed marriage he was 'thunderstruck'. He recorded that he 'retired to mourn with my faithful Sally, groaned all day and several following ones and could eat no pleasant food, nor preach, nor rest, either by night or by day.' Charles was a man of quick and extreme changes of mood but this depression stayed on him longer than usual.

The wedding ceremony was conducted with Wesley in considerable pain. On 10 February he badly sprained his ankle when slipping on some ice. It was not bad enough to stop him preaching but on several occasions he had to preach while kneeling because he couldn't stand for any length of time. He even had to be carried to the Foundery on one occasion so that he could participate in a service.

He married Mrs Vazeille in the middle of February 1751, about a week after he injured his ankle. The precise date is uncertain. He did not record it in his journal and the announcements in different publications gave slightly different dates. It has even been suggested that he married when he did because his ankle made travelling out of the question. Otherwise he may have left it until later.

In today's terminology it seems to have been a case of marriage 'on the rebound', and such marriages often experience strife. The marriage of John and Molly Wesley was no exception.

The newly married couple spent about a week together, then it was back to work for John Wesley. On 4 March, now recovered from his injury, he set off for Bristol. His journal says 'I' not 'we', so presumably Molly was not with him. A week later he presided at the Methodist Conference.

There seem to have been two major problems in their relationship. The main one was that John was determined not to travel a mile less or preach one sermon less in the married state than he would have done when single. That inevitably meant that they would often be apart and at other times she would have to travel with him, bearing the difficulties of travel on horseback in all weathers. What Grace Murray might have tolerated, Molly Wesley would not. She seems to have agreed to it initially, or at least accepted it, and did travel with her husband on occasions. In 1752 she went with him through the north of England and joined him on another tour of Cornwall. She even went to Ireland with him but was greatly troubled by seasickness. Sometimes her daughter, Jenny, accompanied them.

Few people could have lived that kind of itinerant life for long and Molly Wesley was not one of them. John Wesley was wrong to expect it of her.

The second problem was that Mary thought that her husband flirted with other women. Women were attracted to him and he was attracted to them. He also frequently counselled individual Methodists, including women, which often meant that he got closer to other women than was advisable for a married man. In addition, sometimes his actions and words, especially in letters, were open to misinterpretation. Molly saw some of the letters and misinterpreted them. For example, he would write to one of his female followers and refer to love, meaning Christian love. Molly would search his pockets, find the letter before it was despatched, read it and angrily draw the wrong conclusions.

It is probably true to say that John Wesley was naïve in this regard. What may have seemed innocent to him did not always seem innocent to others, especially his wife. Molly became jealous and there was more friction. It also seems that Molly Wesley had a vicious tongue and it was frequently pointed in her husband's direction. She loved to shout and scream and her husband was usually the target of her abuse. Some of Wesley's associates also claimed that she was physically abusive towards him. Did he deserve this treatment? No! Did he cause it? His behaviour was certainly the trigger, if not the cause.

Even as early as four months after the wedding she complained to Charles Wesley about her situation. Charles counselled her, counselled his brother and then spoke to them together. If his words achieved anything, it was only for a short time. The marriage was already sailing on to the rocks. In fact, their marriage was probably doomed before it had started. Wesley expected from her what she was not prepared to give and she expected him to give up what he refused to let go.

In January 1758 Molly came across an un-posted letter from her husband to Sarah Ryan, the housekeeper at Kingswood School. Sarah was a convert who had a dubious past. The letter was spiritual rather than romantic but it was clear that Wesley held Mrs Ryan in high regard. Molly was furious, packed her bags and left, vowing never to return.

But she did return and she continued to read his mail. What was worse she showed his letters to others and gave her biased commentary on them. Their lives continued on; the tensions remained.

In October 1759 he sent her a letter listing the things he disliked about her and asking her to change her ways. Again this shows a degree of naïvety. Such an approach was never likely to do any good, though the letter shows signs of a man who in this regard was rather desperate. He, in fact, listed ten things that he wanted her to amend. A few of his complaints may have been little more than an 18th century man standing up for his position in the home, but most, if true (and it is hard to think that Wesley was lying), indicate that she was a most unpleasant woman. He accused her of reading his private letters, showing them to others, stealing other important papers, lying about him, which included saying that he beat her (there is no evidence of Wesley being violent and it seems contrary to his known conduct), not allowing him any privacy and treating the servants 'like dogs'.

On 23 January 1771 Wesley recorded in his journal that Molly 'set out for Newcastle, purposing "never to return".' Then in Latin he wrote, 'I did not desert her; I did not send her away; I will never recall her.' She went to live in Newcastle and Wesley saw her on occasions when he was in that city. She died in October 1781.

Wesley's marriage and related events were a blot on his life. They damaged his reputation and hurt himself and others, most particularly his wife. While he related to women easily and naturally, he always seemed to get into rough waters when a relationship became serious. And there were no rougher waters than life with Molly Wesley.

Why did he decide to get married when he did? That was probably because of the recent dashing of his hopes with regard to Grace Murray and because of the apparently successful recent marriage of his brother. But why did he marry Mrs Vazeille? That remains a mystery. Whatever the reasons, it was clearly a mistake.

He survived the problems he encountered in his marriage by continuing to immerse himself in his ministry and by adopting a stoical attitude. Amidst these troubles he told Ebenezer Blackwell, 'What a blessing it is to have these little crosses that we may try what spirit we are of! We could not live in continual sunshine.' As far as John Wesley's marriage was concerned there was very little sunshine.

CHAPTER 16

WESLEY AS A WRITER

Not all John Wesley's sermons were specifically evangelistic. He often preached on various aspects of living the Christian life. One of these sermons was on the use of money. It was based on the words of Jesus in Luke 16:9, which read, 'Make to yourselves friends of the mammon of unrighteousness; that, when ye fail, they may receive you into everlasting habitations.'

This sermon contained three principle teachings on money: 'Gain all you can, save all you can and give all you can.' The first two, as those statements stand, were open to misunderstanding but Wesley made their meaning clear. He expected his people to gain what money they could by hard work, honest dealings and without making money a god. By saving Wesley did not mean depositing money into a savings account. He meant not wasting money, not spending it on worthless things, but using it wisely. The third teaching is easy enough to understand: 'Give all you can' to those who need it.

John Wesley's financial practices were consistent with this sermon: he earned, he saved and he gave. His main source of income was from his writings: books and pamphlets. As Methodism developed there was an increasing demand for Wesley's published sermons, various editions of his journal and other writings. He kept back little of the resulting income for his own purposes. He gave most of it away to the work and to those in need.

It is said that one year his income was £30 so he lived on £28 and gave away £2. The next year he received £60 so he lived on £28 and gave away £32. The third year he earned £90 and once more he lived on £28 and gave away £62. He just kept what he needed to live on without falling into debt and gave away the remainder.

Amongst his books were various editions of hymnbooks; different editions of his journal, in which he routinely recorded his travels; and his collected sermons. He also wrote *Primitive Physic* (1747), a book of cures for a variety of medical conditions; *Explanatory Notes on the New Testament* (1755); *A Compendium of Natural Philosophy* (1763); *A Short History of the People Called Methodists* (1765), which is largely extracts from his journal, but with other material added; *A Plain Account of Christian Perfection* (1766), which is not that 'plain'; plus many more works of varying length. He also produced an English translation of the New Testament and brief grammars of English, French, Latin, Greek and Hebrew. Bearing in mind the demanding nature of his many other tasks, his output was remarkable.

Primitive Physic lived up to its name. Today many of its cures sound very primitive. Some were probably little more than quackery, though others, no doubt, were tried and tested. Wesley's great-grand-father, Bartholomew Wes(t)ley, practised medicine, and it may be that some of these remedies came from him. In the 18th century the medical profession itself was generally primitive, and the poor people, and most of Wesley's followers were poor, could not generally afford to avail themselves of professional medical help. Wesley realised that, so he produced this book to meet their needs.

For asthma sufferers he recommended drinking plenty of cold water and having 'a cold bath once a fortnight'. As an alternative, he suggested eating only boiled carrots for a fortnight, which he said 'seldom fails'. To cure baldness, he proposed rubbing 'the part morning or evening with onions, till it is red; and rubbing it afterwards with honey.' A mild burn or scald should be plunged into cold water, or if such was unavailable, it should be electrified (Wesley loved experimenting with electricity). He had three cures for the common cold: drinking 'a pint of cold water [while] lying down in bed'; drinking 'a spoonful of treacle in half a pint of water'; and mixing 'a spoonful of oatmeal and one spoonful of honey, with a little butter, in boiling water, and again, drinking it 'lying down'.

He had several remedies for toothache. These included putting a clove of garlic into the ear, or if that did not work applying the garlic to the tooth; holding a slice of boiled apple between the teeth; gargling with the juice of boiled mulberry leaves; and making a mixture of treacle, nutmeg and three egg yolks, and applying it to the aching tooth. In August 1857, while in Cornwall, he had a bad toothache, which was 'cured' when he rubbed treacle on his cheek.

Wesley also advocated a moderate and light diet, rejecting highly salted and seasoned food, as do many of today's health-conscious people. He argued against eating less than three hours before retiring for the night, and was in favour of early to bed and early to rise. He also urged his readers to get plenty of exercise, especially walking.

When someone launched a stern criticism of Wesley's *Primitive Physic*, the sales of it increased dramatically. Wesley wrote to the critic saying, 'My bookseller informs me that since you published your remarks on *Primitive Physic* there has been greater demand for it than ever. If, therefore, you would please to publish a few further remarks, you would confer a further favour on your humble servant.'

Though Charles Wesley is correctly regarded as the great Methodist hymn writer, John Wesley also wrote hymns. But best are John's translations of German hymns, some of which are magnificent. Perhaps the best is his translation from a piece by Count Zinzendorf, part of which runs,

Jesu, Thy blood and righteousness
My beauty are, my glorious dress;
Midst flaming worlds, in these arrayed,
With joy shall I lift up my head.

Bold shall I stand in Thy great day;
For who aught to my charge shall lay?
Fully absolved through these I am,
From sin and fear, from guilt and shame.

Lord, I believe thy precious blood,
Which at the mercy-seat of God
For ever doth for sinners plead,
For me, even for my soul, was shed.

Or perhaps his translation from Johann Andreas Rothe is even better:

Now I have found the ground wherein
Sure my soul's anchor may remain —
The wounds of Jesus, for my sin
Before the world's foundation slain;
Whose mercy shall unshaken stay,
When heaven and earth are fled away.

Father, Thine everlasting grace
Our scanty thought surpasses far,
Thy heart still melts with tenderness,
Thy arms of love still open are
Returning sinners to receive,
That mercy they may taste and live.

These wonderful translations contain clear biblical imagery and powerful, profound theology, expressed in beautiful poetry that stirs both the mind and the emotions. They are almost other-worldly and in some respects they do take us into that other, better world.

In 1778 he also founded a publication called *The Arminian Magazine*. It later became *The Methodist Magazine* and was one of the longest continually-published magazines in the world. It did not cease publication until 1969.

Wesley also published editions of the books of other writers for his people in a series called *The Christian Library*. This included works by various puritans, books by and about a number of Anglican divines, others by Jonathan Edwards, plus Foxe's *Book of Martyrs*. However, some of these, in the days before copyright controls, he heavily edited. Wesley liked what he thought they should have said, not always what they said. Wesley believed that Methodists should be a reading people. He even told his preachers 'Read or go back to your trade.' If they did not read, they were no good to him as preachers.

CHAPTER 17

NORTH TO SCOTLAND

It would appear that John Wesley was a little nervous about ministering in Scotland. Apart from his ministry in England he had also served in Wales and Ireland. Indeed, one scholar has estimated that he spent about six years of his life in Ireland, first visiting there in 1747. But he did not enter Scotland until April 1751. There were probably two main reasons for his late arrival there. First, the national Church of Scotland was Presbyterian, thus with a different structure and administration from the Church of England, for which Wesley was still a minister. For example, the Scottish church had elders rather than bishops. There was also some tension between the two bodies at this time. Secondly, the Presbyterian Church of Scotland was staunchly Calvinistic. Thus Wesley's brand of Arminianism was not likely to be welcomed there.

George Whitefield though, being a Calvinist, visited Scotland 14 times and preached there with enthusiasm and great success. Whitefield went there first in the summer of 1741. He went again in the middle of the following year during a time of revival and stirred religious enthusiasm to white heat in the second half of that year. During that visit he often preached twice a day and thousands went to hear him, and many were converted. Such was the enthusiasm one evening the service went well into the night and he did not get to bed till 2 am He returned six years later and once more met with success, though not as much as before.

One thing Whitefield noticed in Scotland was that when he

preached he could see and sometimes even hear people leafing through their Bibles. This did not usually happen in other places. It suggested to him that Scotland had a higher percentage of biblically literate people than did other countries where he ministered.

For some years John Wesley seemed content to leave Scotland to the resident Presbyterian ministers, augmented with the occasional visits by Whitefield and others. After all, he had enough to do in the other parts of the British Isles. But in the spring of 1751 he received an invitation to enter Scotland, so he headed north.

He first travelled through the Midlands, visiting earlier trouble spots Wednesbury and Darlaston, where now the people were like 'lambs'. His next port of call was Whitehaven in northern Wales. He preached there three times in one day, and apart from a few stones being thrown early during the second sermon, he was well received. He was delighted with the Methodist society he met there. In two days he spoke with all 240 members of that society and discovered that, with one exception, they were all faithful in attending their class meetings. This he thought 'remarkable', as indeed it was. It was then on to the northern parts of England, including Newcastle, where he stayed at the orphan house.

He crossed the border into Scotland on 24 April and lodged in Musselburgh, near Edinburgh. He appears to have been invited by a career soldier, Captain (later Lt-Col) Bartholomew Gallatin, who was based in that town. Yet he does not seem to have arrived in Scotland with any great hopes. That day he recorded in his journal 'I had no intention to preach in Scotland; nor did I imagine there were any that desired that I should.' But he was wrong. News spread around about the visitor and that evening 'an abundance of people', including some soldiers, gathered to hear him. He preached and they listened attentively, standing like 'statues' until the end of his sermon.

It was then on to Edinburgh, which in Wesley's opinion, was 'one of the dirtiest cities' he had seen. But for whatever reason, (probably not the dirt) he only stayed half a day, before returning to Musselburgh. Oddly, 'a little party of gentlemen' from Edinburgh followed him and engaged him in friendly conversation. He had expected the Scots to be rather reserved or critical but these men 'were as free and open' with Wesley as 'the people of Newcastle and Bristol'.

That second evening in Musselburgh he went to the school where he preached again, this time on 'Seek ye the Lord while he may be found, call ye upon him while he is near.' (Isaiah 55:6) Wesley says that he spoke 'plainly' to them. After the sermon one of the town's Bailies and an elder from the Kirk approached him.

'Mr Wesley', said the elder, 'we would like you to stay for a while. We can find you a grander building to preach in than the school.'

Wesley thought for a moment. The offer was tempting, but Wesley, as always, was on a tight schedule. 'I'm sorry, gentlemen, I can't. Other duties forbid it. I have a conference to attend in Leeds and other pressing responsibilities.' He paused for a moment. 'But I'll do my best to send one of my preachers instead.'

The two Scots were disappointed, but accepted the evangelist's offer.

A little later Wesley arranged to send one of his younger men, Christopher Hopper, to Scotland in his place. Hopper was an ideal choice. He came from a little south of the Scottish border, and was an able and zealous preacher.

There are numerous hints in Wesley's journal of this period that suggest he expected to suffer considerable opposition on doctrinal grounds from the Scots but on this trip there had been none. Rather, they supported and encouraged him.

He then travelled south and visited his old home territory at Epworth. But the Methodist society in that town was not in good order. Some Methodist preachers had spread rumours about Wesley, which the Epworth Methodists had been all too ready to believe. In addition, some had rejected Methodist doctrine, while others had turned their backs on Methodist rules of conduct. To Wesley it seemed that the Epworth Methodists were 'poor, dead and senseless'. His time there on this occasion was short and unhappy.

A couple of days later the weather turned nasty. Heavy rain blanketed northern England. Wesley was trying to get to Leeds when he heard that the coach destined for York had overturned in the flood waters nearby, tipping the occupants into the river. Mercifully no one was hurt, but all the travellers were shaken and soaked.

Wesley and his companion took a different route. The rain tumbled down, making the ground treacherous, which caused their horses to stumble at times, and poor visibility made finding their way difficult. Eventually, they met up with some other travellers who knew the area well and they were able to cross the river without too much difficulty.

In Leeds 30 preachers gathered for what Wesley called a 'little conference', that is, a conference that lasted just one day. As usual, John Wesley dominated it. But he was encouraged by the response of all but one of the men who assembled on that occasion. By this time he was experienced and realistic enough to accept that as a reasonable result.

Wesley had a great influence on a man named Thomas Hanby (1733-96). He lived in Durham in the far north of England and became a leading Methodist in Scotland. His father was a drunkard and this led to the neglect of Thomas and his two siblings. Bad became worse when both his parents died while he was still young. He then went to live with an aunt and was confirmed in the Anglican Church.

He had his first contact with Methodists in his teens. He went along with some friends to a meeting of a Methodist society simply to mock its people, but he found something strangely attractive about them. He went back the next night, and again and again, but then joined another Christian group for a while.

John Wesley arrived in Barnard Castle, Hanby's home town, in May 1752 and Hanby went along to hear him. The meeting turned into another riot, with one group commandeering the fire engine and dowsing the congregation with water. Hanby and some friends tried to stop it but they were hopelessly outnumbered. The mischief went on and Wesley had to retreat.

In spite of having much contact with Christian people, Hanby still remained unconverted. But what he had heard from Wesley and others had sunk deep into his soul and would not go away. He prayed and prayed again. When he had finished praying he prayed once more, this time in 'a dark place'. So dark was it that he was 'greatly terrified for fear' that he would 'see the devil' – but instead he met Christ.

His Christian experience quickly deepened and he began to feel a desire to preach. But, he wondered, was this desire from God or was it from the devil? He continued on in this state of indecision for some days. He them went to visit a dying woman whom he did not know. He stood at the back of the little group surrounding her bed. But she noticed him and called out, 'Young man, God has called you to preach the gospel; you have long rejected the call, but He will make you go. Obey the call! Obey the call!'

Hanby was stunned. How could this woman have known of his inward struggle? But this came to him as a word from God and he obeyed the call. He went to the local chapel the following Sunday morning and the expected preacher failed to appear. The people urged Hanby to take his place. Now the doubts were gone, so he did. What's more he preached again that afternoon and again that evening.

Soon after this he began to itinerate in the Midlands, visiting Birmingham, Wednesbury, Ashbourne (later the birth place of Catherine Booth of The Salvation Army) and numerous other towns. On a number of occasions he encountered violent opposition as he preached. In one of these incidents a powerfully built man, a highly successful boxer, emerged from the crowd. Hanby feared the worst but the boxer threw a protective arm around him and hurried him through the crowd and to the outskirts of the town, with the mob in pursuit. The pugilist then shouted 'Run!' So Hanby ran. The boxer followed behind him, beating away any troublemakers that came close. Hanby managed to escape and hid behind the hedges in a field for the night. But further dangers awaited him in many places during the following months.

In 1755 the Methodist Conference officially accepted him as travelling preacher. He was appointed to Canterbury in Kent, in the southeast of England, and shortly before he arrived there he was set upon by two soldiers who robbed him. Soldiers were plentiful in Canterbury at that time as rumours still abounded about the possibility of an invasion from France. The word quickly got around about the preacher who had been robbed, and when he appeared in the open air to preach to them, hundreds listened intently.

A Methodist society of about 10 existed in Canterbury when he arrived. When he left some months later there were 60. Afterwards he ministered in different parts of Scotland, the north of England, the Midlands, the south-east again and the south-west.

In 1794 he was appointed the fourth President of the Methodist Conference, Wesley by that time was dead. Hanby died late in December 1796. His last words were, 'I have fought the good fight.' And so he had. He had been a travelling preacher for over 40 years.

***

In April 1753 Wesley made a return visit to Scotland. Once more heavy rain fell and this time his horse became bogged in the mud. It was only with great difficulty that he and his companion released the poor beast from its predicament and they were able to continue on their way.

This time he was more intent on conducting ministry in Scotland than he had been on his earlier visit. He passed through Dumfries and Thorny Hill and went on to Glasgow. He preached just outside the town on the second morning but the weather was foul, with a very strong wind, and few came to listen. That afternoon they erected a tent on the same site and Wesley tried again. On this occasion 'six times' as many people turned up to listen. It was a bigger crowd but one much smaller than he had attracted in such places as Moorfields and Newcastle.

The next day the weather was again bad and the local clergyman invited Wesley to preach in his church. This surprised Wesley but he seized the opportunity. That afternoon the weather abated a little and as the crowd gathered it became apparent that they would not all fit into the church, so he preached in the church grounds. The following Sunday he again preached out of doors. This time on 'This is life eternal, to know thee, the only true God, and Jesus Christ whom thou hast sent.' (John 17:3) Even though it 'rained much' there were about a thousand present. Later that day he ministered in the prison.

One major Scottish convert to the ranks of the Methodists was Duncan Wright (1736-91). He had been born in Perthshire into a nominal Presbyterian family and joined the army at the age of 18. The military stationed him in Limerick in Ireland. His mother died soon after his arrival there and he felt that in some measure he had caused her death by leaving her when she was ill.

He began to read avidly to take his mind off his troubles. At first it was mainly plays and novels, but he later turned to theology. Halfway through one theological volume he became convinced that he was 'a lost sinner' and that he needed Christ. But for a while, his searchings for Him proved fruitless.

He became aware of the Methodists but at first hesitated to attend any of their meetings, because they were 'objects of universal contempt' in the area, though Wright 'hardly knew what to make of them.'

But at the end of 1755, rather hesitantly, he went along to see for himself and then began to attend their meetings regularly. A few months later he was converted.

Being a Christian of any kind in the army was not easy but being a Methodist was worse. Even the 'tender mercies' of his fellow soldiers 'were cruel'. His commanding officer particularly had a dislike for Methodists, but when he became aware that the little group that Wright assembled around him behaved themselves he accepted the situation. In fact, Wright was promoted to the rank of sergeant. He also began to preach.

John Wesley, who had previously met Wright, heard about his efforts as a preacher and minister to his class of soldiers, and wrote to tell him that if he left the army, there was a place for him amongst the Methodist preachers. Wright's health deteriorated and towards the end of 1764 he was discharged from the army.

But the following year he joined a new army. He became the preacher for the Waterford Methodist circuit. John Wesley had his eye on him and soon invited him to accompany him on some of his travels. For a year he did that but his health broke down again. Upon recovery, he returned to circuit work and eventually went back to Scotland.

In his native Scotland he found his calling. He preached in both English and Gaelic and hundreds listened attentively to, as he put it, his 'blundering preaching'. But 'blundering' or not, many of his hearers listened as 'still as night' and some cried tears of repentance.

Alexander Mather (1733-1800) was another of the handful of Scottish preachers amongst Wesley's men, though his ministry was more outside Scotland than in it. He was brought up in a godly home in Brechin near the eastern coast of Scotland. In his teens he was nearly killed in a boating accident, when a horse on board panicked and jumped into the river, taking Alexander and the two boatmen with it, leaving his mother and another man the only ones still on board. He held on to the horse's reins and was dragged near to the bank and was eventually helped, with some difficulty, on to dry land.

He moved to London in 1752 and to his surprise met a young Scottish woman who had been a companion in his early childhood. They soon married. Mather had vowed that when he married he would conduct family devotions but in the excitement of his new life this was forgotten. But his wife became ill, which drove him to prayer, and eventually he fulfilled his vow and prayed with her. However, it was not clear that either were yet converted. Alexander may have been but his wife almost certainly was not.

The next year he was put out of work and walked London's streets looking for employment. Almost by chance he met a baker named Marriott and asked him for a job. Marriott looked him over, liked what he saw and employed him.

Thomas Marriott and his wife were members of the Methodist Society that met at the Foundery. The Mathers then joined that society. One week they heard a sermon from John Nelson, who had been converted in Moorfields at the beginning of John Wesley's itinerant ministry. The following week they heard Charles Wesley. These addresses made them both think.

In the spring of 1754 John Wesley returned to London and the Mathers went to hear him. Wesley was unwell, but preached none-the-less. His text was 'now for a season, if need be ye are in heaviness through manifold temptations.' (1 Peter 1:6) It was the right text for that moment. The Mathers knew all about 'manifold temptations' and the 'heaviness' they cause. The words seemed especially designed for their condition.

Wesley's voice was less powerful than usual, but his message carried the Spirit's power. By the time Wesley had finished, the doubts that had long confronted the Mathers had been washed away. They knew they were born again.

Mather later approached John Wesley about becoming a Methodist preacher. Wesley never made the way sound easy. He warned Mather that 'To be a Methodist preacher is not the way to ease, honour, pleasure or profit. It is a life of much labour and reproach.'

No doubt Mather already knew that, but such difficulties were not going to deter him. He responded, 'I have no desire to engage therein unless it is the call of God. But I am prepared to suffer in doing the will of God.'

Wesley was impressed, put him on trial and he became a Methodist circuit preacher. He served in the Epworth circuit, which then included the towns Grimsby and Sheffield. Later he led the Newcastle circuit, which at that time included the Scottish town Musselburgh. Being so far north also gave him opportunity to preach in Brechin, his home town. Mather proved very able and he became an advisor to Wesley and a leading figure in the blossoming Methodist movement. The year after John Wesley's death, Mather became the President of the Methodist Conference.

Overall, Scotland did not prove to be a successful mission field for Methodism. In later years Wesley visited there fairly often, as did some of his preachers, but success was limited. In fact many of the converts they did make attached themselves to the local Kirks, rather than a Methodist society. There were pockets where the Methodist message was accepted by a reasonable number, such as Aberdeen, Dundee, Edinburgh and Perth. But in most of Scotland the Methodism of John Wesley, Thomas Hanby, Duncan Wright and Alexander Mather did not take hold.

CHAPTER 18

IS THIS DEATH?

It is not every man who writes his own epitaph but John Wesley did. What is more, he did it nearly 38 years before he died.

He made another visit to Cornwall in the summer of 1753. While there he was taken ill. It started with his nose bleeding badly. This was followed by a severe bout of diarrhoea, which lasted several days and was later accompanied by a headache, violent vomiting and cramp in his feet and legs. At one stage he ate nothing for a day and a half, just drinking claret and water. In all, the sickness lasted about 12 days. His condition was bad enough to restrict his travel and preaching a little during that period, but not by much.

Soon after this he received an invitation to preach in a meeting house in Plymouth Dock, built for George Whitefield. He rejoiced that the invitation and his acceptance of it trampled on 'bigotry and party-zeal'. In fact, he thought, 'Ought not all who love God to love one another?' Wesley and Whitefield may have disagreed on some doctrines but they were still preachers of the same Saviour and they both knew it.

Through early autumn he was in better health and was able to continue his energetic mission, travelling eastward, with little interruption. He did, however, have five days rest in London in the middle of October. He probably took the rest because he was not feeling completely well, for almost as soon as he took up work again he was sick once more.

On Saturday 20 he felt 'out of order'. The next day he 'was considerably worse, but could not think of sparing' himself as a congregation awaited him. On the Monday he 'rose extremely sick' yet in the afternoon he set off for Canterbury to keep a preaching engagement scheduled for the next day. On the way he was 'obliged to stop' at Welling when he became too sick to continue, and for the same reason stopped again just outside Chatham. In spite of his condition he preached that evening and the next morning at seven. He then completed the journey to Canterbury, where he was so ill, with what appears to have been a fever, that he had to go to bed.

For a few days he felt better, but in the middle of November he again had a fever with a bad cough. He was clearly ill, as he had been for some time, though he often seemed to prefer ignoring it.

At the end of that month he retreated to Lewisham, which was then just outside London, in hope of recovery. But he seems to have thought that his chances were not too good, for he wrote down what he wanted on his tombstone. It read:

Here lieth the Body
Of
JOHN WESLEY
A brand plucked out of the burning,
Who died of consumption in the fifty-first year of his age
Not leaving, after his debts are paid,
Ten pounds behind him,
Praying,
'God be merciful to me, an unprofitable servant.'

His brother Charles hurried to his side, and in some measure, took his place as the leader of Methodism, visiting societies and preaching when John was too unwell to do so. However, both brothers knew that that would not last long, as Charles, because of his marriage, had much reduced his itinerancy.

Though John Wesley stopped travelling for much of December and the early months of the following year were also quiet, it did not stop him working. He filled much of that time by starting to write his *Notes on the New Testament*. This and his published sermons became Methodist doctrinal standards. At about this time he also edited some books for his Christian Library. What travel he did undertake during this period was usually by carriage, which Wesley called 'the machine', rather than on horseback.

Also in the first half of 1754 he preached only occasionally. Indeed, he did not preach at all for four months at the end of 1753 and the beginning of the next year. Even his voice had lost much of its power, which remained a problem when he did recommence preaching. During those months he was still unwell. He even wrote in his journal less often. He was, however, able to attend that year's conference in May. Only death would stop him missing that. It was probably not until 1755 that he was fully well again, or, at least, nearly so. But even in the middle of December that year he had a relapse and felt ill again but soon recovered.

He returned to Wednesbury that April. The people there had been savage lions in 1743, roaring violently at anything Methodist, and lambs in 1751. This time a 'great congregation assembled' to hear him and there was no trouble. That evening he met with the society and 'a solemn awe seemed to run all through the company.' Wesley said in his journal, 'We have indeed preached the Gospel here "with much contention". But the success overpays the labour'. The Methodists of Wednesbury had been through the furnace but had emerged a holy people.

The conference in 1755 was held in Leeds early in May. It was to be an important conference. The major item on the agenda was 'Whether we ought to separate from the Church' of England. A number of lay Methodist preachers had begun to administer the sacraments, which was against Church of England Canon Law, which declared that only an ordained minister could do so, and it was also against John Wesley's wishes. But not all Methodists felt comfortable going to their local church for the Lord's Supper. They would rather take it in a Methodist meeting-house, even if it meant a layman administered it. This raised the whole issue of whether or not Methodism should remain in the Church of England. It had become a hot topic and it had to be dealt with.

Not that this was a new issue. It had been discussed at the first Methodist Conference in 1744 but it had been quickly dismissed then. But now, eleven years later, the issue had become more relevant and more difficult.

In preparation for that conference debate John and Charles Wesley read together *A Gentleman's Reasons for his Dissent from the Church of England*. This book was written by a dissenting minister named Towgood who lived in Exeter in the south-west of England. The Wesleys were not impressed. John found the book 'an elaborate and lively tract', but felt that the writer had dipped his pen 'in vinegar and gall'. Indeed, it was a 'most saucy and virulent satire' upon the church.

In this conference debate John Wesley seems to have allowed his preachers to have their say more than was usually the case. In fact, he recorded in his journal, 'we [presumably the Wesley brothers] desired all the preachers to speak their minds'. He knew it was a divisive issue and trying to silence its advocates would not make it go away. This decision may also suggest that he had doubts about the right road to take.

The debate was prolonged and at times heated, but the result appears to have been a little inconclusive. However, John Wesley felt that the general view was that even though it may have been 'lawful' to separate, it was not 'expedient', though this may reflect his own stand rather than being the view of the majority of conference delegates. Either way, Methodism remained, at least for the time being, part of the Church of England.

In the days that immediately followed that conference Wesley encountered some opposition to that decision. He was relieved that in one place he found that fewer than he expected were 'prejudiced against the church', though those dissidents still numbered about 40, so it was not a number that could be ignored. Yet most, if not all, of the laymen who had administered the Lord's Supper ceased to do so.

But it was a strange situation. In some respects Methodism was functioning from within the Church of England, but in other respects from outside it. It was a relationship that was always going to break at some stage. But that fracture was years ahead. The Wesley brothers would continue as ministers of that church for the remainder of their lives.

A few days later he wrote in his journal, 'We rode (my wife and I) to Northallerton.' But the next day it was 'I rode on to Newcastle.' Molly does not seem to have been happy.

In the middle of the year Wesley made an assessment of what God had done through him and his colleagues since his return from Georgia. He noted the great works of God carried out in America and Scotland during that period, but thought that the revival in England had been even more remarkable. The features he mentioned were: 'The numbers of persons on whom God has wrought; the swiftness of his work in many, both convinced and truly converted in a few days; the depth of it in most of these, changing the heart as well as the whole conversation [the whole behaviour]; the clearness of it, enabling them boldly to say, "Thou hast loved me; though hast given thyself for me" the continuance of it' over a period of more than 17 years, 'without any observable intermission'. Though there had been highs and lows, it had, indeed, been an ongoing and amazing work of God. And John Wesley was still very much alive.

CHAPTER 19

WESTWARD AGAIN

Methodism was progressing well in south-western England. Opposition still existed but it did little to quench Methodist fire. There were strongholds in Bristol, Plymouth and numerous Cornish towns and villages. Wesley visited the south-west again in August and September 1755 hoping to further strengthen the work. Wherever he preached people came from a wide area to hear him.

In St Mewan in Cornwall he had the largest attendance he could recall in that place. The next day he preached in a packed meeting house in St Austell and that evening he proclaimed the word in St Ewe. At St Ewe 'one or two felt the edge of God's sword and sunk to the ground'. The atmosphere was electric. 'It seemed' to Wesley that no one there 'would escape' God. Indeed, that evening the Lord 'both heard and answered prayer', many being touched by the Gospel message.

The next day he rode to Redruth, where he found a 'congregation' waiting in the open air for him. He was warmly welcomed by the local Methodists, but in the excitement no one thought to offer him any food or drink. He was tired after the journey, but as soon as he began to preach the tiredness dropped from him. That night he reflected, 'Surely God is in this place also.'

The next day, a Sunday, he preached at 8 am on 'How shall I give thee up, Ephraim?' (Hosea 11:8) He later recorded that 'Many' of his listeners 'endeavoured, but in vain, to hide their tears.' The word of

God was striking home.

That afternoon he went to Gwennap pit. This pit formed a natural amphitheatre, a 'round green hollow, gently shelving down' more than 15 metres deep. It is thought to have been created by subsidence caused by copper mining, and, with its sloping ground and massive size, was ideal for preaching out of doors. Wesley estimated that it stretched 60 metres one way and 90 the other. It could hold thousands and its excellent acoustics meant that all could hear him. Wesley called it 'the finest' preaching spot of its type 'in the kingdom'.

On this occasion 'several thousand' listened to the message. As Wesley finished the storm clouds moved in. Then the rain poured down, but by then the people were dispersing. He was to revisit Gwennap many times.

It was not unusual for Wesley to attend church services in which he did not preach. On his next visit to Redruth he attended the Anglican church, in which the minister 'preached an excellent sermon'. During the service, a woman, who had been giggling in the earlier part of the service, cried out 'several times', fell down and was carried out of the church. What happened to her after that appears to be unrecorded.

Soon after that he left Cornwall and went through Devon and on to Bristol. There he took a break from travelling and finished writing his *Notes on the New Testament*. When he did re-engage in preaching he found the people of Bristol quiet and attentive. 'No rudeness is now at Bristol', he later wrote. When he interviewed the members of the local Methodist society he was pleased that most of them seemed genuinely devoted to God. But Bristol was not a reformed city, as shall be seen.

He returned to London for a while to minister to his people there. On 5 November George Whitefield visited him. It was a wonderful reunion. 'Disputings are now no more', Wesley recalled. 'We love one another, and join hand in hand to promote the cause of our common Master.' The differences still existed, but the arguing over them had, for the most part, ended.

A couple of days before Christmas 1755 Wesley found himself in the robe-chamber next to the House of Lords in London. Why Wesley was there is unclear but he was present when the aging King George II was putting on his robes. Wesley noted that the king's 'brow was much furrowed with age, and quite clouded with care' and his 'blanket of ermine' was 'so heavy and cumbersome' that he had difficulty moving. Wesley wondered, 'is this all the world can give even to a king? Alas what a bauble is human greatness! And even this will not endure,' Yet Wesley seems to have had a high regard for this king, probably because of his opposition to the Catholic-inspired Jacobite rebellions. He once wrote in his journal 'we love King George', and when the king died in 1760 Wesley wondered, 'When will England have a better prince?'

Early in March 1756 Wesley returned to Bristol. He found it 'all in a flame', though the cause was politics not religion. It was the lead up to a by-election. Bristol in those days had two members of parliament, one of whom had recently died, hence the election. At that time not all adults had the vote, not even all the men, and there appears to have been a violent dispute between different groups and also trouble over who should stand for the two parties.

When Wesley arrived on the scene he had a cold and had lost his voice, so he was unable to speak publicly. He did, however, interview a number of that Methodist society individually and urged each to behave in a Christian manner throughout the crisis.

Many years later he urged his people 'To vote, without fee or reward, for the person they judged most worthy. To speak no evil of the person they voted against' and 'to take care their spirits were not sharpened against those who voted on the other side'. He did not mention voting for a particular party, though he had his preference. Wesley's voting policy is wise Christian advice for any voter.

From Bristol he ventured into Wales and on to Trevecca, where he met Howell Harris. Howell Harris was a great Welsh preacher who had long exercised a successful ministry. He was unwell when Wesley arrived, so he was quite happy for Wesley to do the preaching on this occasion. As it happened Wesley's arrival was on the same day as the meeting of the local justices and commissioners. When Wesley preached they assembled to hear him, making up a congregation richer and more polite than many Wesley spoke to. Later he wrote in his journal that he hoped that 'one or two' of them 'may lay' his spoken words 'to heart'.

Two days later he preached to a rougher congregation, made up of people who had gathered from around that district. His subject was salvation by faith, from Ephesians 2:8. 'All the blessings which God hath bestowed upon man are of his mere grace, bounty or favour; his free, undeserved favour,' he began.

> It was free grace that 'formed man of the dust of the ground, and breathed into him a living soul,' and stamped on that soul the image of God, and 'put all things under his feet.' The same free grace continues to us, at this day, life and breath, and all things. For there is nothing we are, or have, or do, which can deserve the least thing at God's hand. 'All our works, Thou, O God, hast wrought in us' [Isaiah 26:12], and whatever righteousness may be found in man, this is also the gift of God.

> Wherewithal then shall a sinful man atone for any the least of his sins? With his own works? No! Were they ever so many or holy, they are not his own, but God's. But indeed they are all unholy and sinful themselves, so that every one of them needs a fresh atonement. Only corrupt fruit grows on a corrupt tree. And his heart is altogether corrupt and abominable; being 'come short of the glory of God'. Therefore, having nothing, neither righteousness nor works, to plead his mouth is utterly stopped before God.

If then sinful men find favour with God, it is 'grace upon grace!' If God vouchsafe still to pour fresh blessings upon us, yea, the greatest of all blessings, salvation; what can we say to these things, but 'Thanks be unto God for his unspeakable gift!' And thus it is. 'God commendeth his love toward us, in that, while we were yet sinners, Christ died' to save us.' 'By grace' then 'are ye saved through faith'. Grace is the source, faith the condition, of salvation.

He then explored the nature of the faith that saves and the salvation that it leads to. He first spoke of wrong kinds of faith. The faith that saves is not 'the faith of a heathen', nor is it 'the faith of a devil', who knows the reality of God, but does not know Him as Saviour and Lord. Rather saving faith 'is a faith in Christ; Christ, and God through Christ, are the proper objects of it. For thus saith the Scripture, "With the heart man believeth unto righteousness;" and, "If thou shalt confess with thy mouth the Lord Jesus, and shalt believe in thy heart that God hath raised him from the dead, thou shalt be saved".' (Romans 10:9-10)

As he spoke on this occasion there was little disturbance. The wind was blustery and cold, but few went away. Indeed, as he preached more came to listen. He continued,

At this time, more especially, will we speak, that 'by grace are ye saved through faith'. Nothing but this can give a check to that immorality which hath 'overspread the land as a flood'. Let the 'righteousness which is of God by faith' be brought in, and so shall its proud waves be stayed. Nothing but this can stop the mouths of those who 'glory in their shame, and openly deny the Lord that bought them.' They can talk as sublimely of the law as he that hath it written by God in his heart. To hear them speak on this head might incline one to think they were not far from the kingdom of God: but take them out of the law into the gospel;

begin with the righteousness of faith; with Christ, 'the end of the law to everyone that believeth'; and those who but now appeared almost, if not altogether, Christians, stand confessed the sons of perdition; as far from life and salvation (God be merciful unto them!) as the depth of hell from the height of heaven.

For this reason the Adversary so rages whenever 'salvation by faith' is declared to the world; for this reason did he stir up earth and hell to destroy those who first preached it. And for the same reason, knowing that faith alone could overturn the foundations of his kingdom, did he call forth all his forces, and employ all his lies to affright Martin Luther from reviving it. Go forth then, thou little child that believest in Him in weakness. Though thou art helpless and weak as an infant of days, the strong man shall not be able to stand before thee.

Now, thanks be to God, which giveth us the victory through our Lord Jesus Christ; to whom, with the Father and the Holy Ghost, be blessing, and glory, and wisdom, and thanksgiving, and honour, and power, and might, forever and ever. Amen.

When he had finished the people dispersed, but a few remained behind to speak to Wesley and his helpers.

CHAPTER 20

'YOU MUST BE BORN AGAIN'

Wesley's plan was to go on another visit to Ireland, which meant first travelling north with his companions to Holyhead to catch the boat. But when they woke up the following day winter had returned. The whole area was covered in snow and more was falling. But Wesley's policy was not to be deterred by the weather unless it was completely unmanageable, so off they set in a northward direction. The conditions were difficult and dangerous. Wesley had travelled that way before, but now it all seemed so different, just a blanket of white over hills and valleys. Treacherous terrain was hidden by the snow and the horses often missed their footing.

When the afternoon arrived the snows began to melt. Then hail pelted down. Next the hail stopped and the rain poured upon them. Wesley had journeyed through all weathers in his ministry but rarely had conditions been more difficult.

They pushed on to Dolgellau in the foothills of Snowdonia and spent the night in the local inn. It had been a tiring and difficult day, but when time came to retire, sleep did not come. A noisy group of sailors had rented the room beneath them and made sure that their festivities continued on till the early hours of the morning. They sang, they shouted, they celebrated, though what they were celebrating was far from clear. This gave the preachers little chance of gaining the rest they needed. But they were still up a little before six the next morning, which was late for Wesley.

It was then on to Holyhead, once more in bleak conditions. Inevitably, it seemed, they arrived later than planned and were told that the packet boat to Ireland had already departed. However, the weather turned bad again, and the boat was forced back to Holyhead. There was a terrible storm on their first night there and conditions did not improve much during the next few days.

They made the best of their time. That Sunday morning they met with a few of the local people and expounded the Scriptures to them. Mid-afternoon they attended the local 'evening' service. Then Wesley returned to his accommodation where he found a group of people eager to listen to him. He preached from Luke 21:36, warning his hearers to be continually on the watch for they did not know when the Son of Man, Jesus Christ, would return.

The next day they departed for Ireland and arrived in Dublin the following day. Rumours of an invasion by the French hung over his time there, though the people did not seem too concerned.

On Good Friday he met with the society in Dublin and was delighted to see that it now numbered nearly 400 men and women. He led them in a service of covenant renewal, during which 'Many mourned before God, and many were comforted.' (Wesley commonly used the word mourn for repentance.) The following week he met the Irish Methodist preachers and was pleased with their sense of unity.

He moved on and eventually came to Portarlington, near the centre of the country. In the morning he preached in the local assembly room, where 'many of the best in the town' had gathered. His text was 'Ye must be born again' (John 3:7), which came as a bit of a shock to many in his congregation. He did not mince his words but they listened intently.

When he had finished the room was silent, or nearly so. A few dried their eyes with handkerchiefs. Most stood and left the building but some stayed behind to ask more about the new birth.

A few days later Wesley journeyed to Clonmell further south, which he thought 'the pleasantest town' he had seen in Ireland. There he had the unusual experience of preaching in a large loft, capable, he thought, of holding over 500 people. However it was not full and many that were present seemed a little anxious. At first Wesley was unsure why there was this sense of uncertainty. Then he found out that the safety of the loft was in doubt, as another such loft in a nearby town had recently collapsed under the weight of a few hundred people and word about that had reached Clonmell.

In the middle of July he arrived at Tullamore in central Ireland. Early in the evening he went out to preach, taking his stand on a street corner. He and his companions began by singing a hymn, which encouraged a few to come close to listen, while others stood in the doorways of their houses. When the Methodists had finished singing, there was a gentle whisper from those assembled, asking each other 'What's next?'

But when Wesley began to speak the people listened silently. Once more he preached on the new birth. It had become a common theme for Wesley, as it had for George Whitefield. He read a few verses from John chapter three, made a brief introduction and then asked, 'Why must we be born again? What is the foundation of this doctrine?' He answered,

> The foundation of it lies near as deep as the creation of the world; in the scriptural account whereof we read, 'And God,' the three-one God, 'said, "Let us make man in our image, after our likeness." So God created man in his own image, in the image of God created he him' (Genesis 1:26-27), a spiritual being, endued with understanding, freedom of will and various affections. It was not merely in his political image, the governor of this lower world, having 'dominion over the fishes of the sea, and over all the earth.' It was chiefly in his moral image; which, according to the Apostle, is 'righteousness and true holiness'. (Ephesians 4:24) In

this image of God was man made. 'God is love.'

Accordingly, man at his creation was full of love; which was the sole principle of all his tempers, thoughts, words and actions. God is full of justice, mercy and truth; so was man as he came from the hands of his Creator. God is spotless purity; and so man was in the beginning pure from every sinful blot; otherwise God could not have pronounced him, as well as all the other work of his hands, 'very good' (Genesis 1:31). This he could not have been, had he not been pure from sin, and filled with righteousness and true holiness. For there is no medium, if we suppose an intelligent creature not to love God, not to be righteous and holy, we necessarily suppose him not to be good at all; much less to be 'very good'.

The people were listening and more were coming out of their houses to see what was going on. Some soldiers appeared and joined the increasing crowd. Wesley, as usual, ignored the movement and continued on.

However, man was created able to stand and yet liable to fall. And this God himself apprised him of and gave him a solemn warning against it. Nevertheless, man did not abide in honour: He fell from his high estate. He 'ate of the tree whereof the Lord had commanded him, "Thou shalt not eat thereof".' By this wilful act of disobedience to his Creator, this flat rebellion against his Sovereign, he openly declared that he would no longer have God to rule over him.

Now, God had told him before, 'In the day that thou eatest' of that fruit, 'thou shalt surely die'. And the word of the Lord cannot be broken. Accordingly, in that day he did die: He died to God – the most dreadful of all deaths.

And in Adam all died, all human kind, all the children of men who were then in Adam's loins. The natural consequence of this is that every one descended from him comes into the world spiritually dead, dead to God, wholly dead in sin. That is, entirely void of the life of God; void of the image of God, of all that righteousness and holiness wherein Adam was created. Instead of this, every man born into the world now bears the image of the devil in pride and self-will; the image of the beast, in sensual appetites and desires. This, then, is the foundation of the new birth: the entire corruption of our nature. Hence it is, that, being born in sin, we must be 'born again'. Hence every one that is born of a woman must be born of the Spirit of God.

But how must a man be born again? The precise manner how it begins and ends, rises and falls, no man can tell. A man may be born from above, born of God, born of the Spirit, in a manner which bears a very near analogy to the natural birth.

Without warning, a large, powerfully-built man burst through the crowd. He screamed in drunken anger. He shouted at Wesley. 'You lie; you lie.'

He shouted at the people, 'Go from here! Don't listen to this man. He lies. He lies, I tell you.'

The preacher was forced to stop speaking. The man moved towards Wesley menacingly, but Wesley looked him straight in the eye. Suddenly the man stopped and, mid-curse, removed his hat and then retreated to hide behind some others in the crowd.

Wesley took advantage of the regained silence and began speaking again. He recapped a little on what he had said and then continued on.

And this is the truth. While a man is in a mere natural state, before he is born of God, he has, in a spiritual sense, eyes and sees not; a thick impenetrable veil lies upon them. He has ears, but hears not; he is utterly deaf to what he is most of all concerned to hear. His other spiritual senses are all locked up: He is in the same condition as if he had them not. Hence he has no knowledge of God; no intercourse with Him. He is not at all acquainted with Him.

But as soon as he is born of God, there is a total change in all these particulars. The 'eyes of his understanding are opened', and he sees 'the light of the glory of God'. His ears being opened, he is now capable of hearing the inward voice of God, saying, 'Be of good cheer; thy sins are forgiven thee' – 'go and sin no more.'

He is now alive to God through Jesus Christ. He lives a life which the world knoweth not of, a 'life which is hid with Christ in God'. God is continually breathing, as it were, upon the soul; and his soul is breathing unto God. Grace is descending into his heart; and prayer and praise ascending to heaven: And by this intercourse between God and man, this fellowship with the Father and the Son, as by a kind of spiritual respiration, the life of God in the soul is sustained; and the child of God grows up, till he comes to the 'full measure of the stature of Christ'.

From hence we can see the nature of the new birth. It is that great change which God works in the soul when He brings it into life; when He raises it from the death of sin to the life of righteousness. It is the change wrought in the whole soul by the almighty Spirit of God when it is 'created anew in Christ Jesus'; when it is 'renewed after the image of God, in righteousness and true holiness.'

Be you baptized or unbaptized, 'you must be born again'; otherwise it is not possible you should be inwardly holy; and without inward as well as outward holiness, you cannot be happy, even in this world, much less in the world to come.

Do you say, 'Nay, but I do no harm to any man; I am honest and just in all my dealings; I do not curse, or take the Lord's name in vain. I do not profane the Lord's day. I am no drunkard. I do not slander my neighbour, nor live in any wilful sin.' If this be so, it were much to be wished that all men went as far as you do. But you must go farther yet, or you cannot be saved: still 'you must be born again'? Do you add, 'I do go farther yet; for I not only do no harm, but do all the good I can'? I doubt that fact; I fear you have had a thousand opportunities of doing good which you have suffered to pass by unimproved, and for which therefore you are accountable to God. But if you had improved them all, if you really had done all the good you possibly could to all men, yet this does not at all alter the case; still 'you must be born again'. Without this nothing will do any good to your poor, sinful, polluted soul.

'Nay,' you say, 'I constantly attend all the ordinances of God: I keep to my church and sacrament.' It is well you do: But all this will not keep you from hell, except you be born again. Go to church twice a day; go to the Lord's table every week; say ever so many prayers in private; hear ever so many good sermons; read ever so many good books, still 'you must be born again'. None of these things will stand in the place of the new birth.

Let this therefore, if you have not already experienced this inward work of God, be your continual prayer: 'Lord, add this to all thy blessings – let me be born again! Deny whatever thou pleasest, but deny not this; let me be "born from above"! Take away whatsoever seemeth thee good: reputation, fortune, friends, health, only give me this, to be born of the Spirit, to be received among the children of God! Amen!'

When he had finished most of the people soon went back into their homes. A few stayed to talk but not many. The concept of being born again was alien to Nicodemus, alien to many in Wesley's time and alien to many today. But the fact remains: you must be born again.

***

On Sunday 13 March 1757 Wesley made an entry in his journal, which on its own sounds of no great consequence. It did, however, record what came to be an important encounter. Wesley wrote, 'as soon as I had done preaching, Mr Fletcher came, who had just been ordained priest, and hastened to the chapel on purpose to assist, as he supposed me to be alone.' A week later he wrote, 'Mr Fletcher helped me again.' Fletcher's sudden appearance was especially timely as John Wesley had been feeling unwell again and had prayed to God for a helper. As it happens, in the years ahead John Fletcher (1729-85) was to be a great help to the Wesleys and Methodism, so God answered that prayer in an ongoing way.

Apart from his brother, and George Whitefield in the early years, this saintly John Fletcher was John Wesley's greatest helper. Fletcher was born in Switzerland and had been christened Jean de la Fléchère. He moved to England in 1750 and tutored the sons of a Member of the British Parliament. He met John Wesley in 1752 and corresponded with him. He was converted early in 1755 and entered the Anglican ministry two years later.

Fletcher's native tongue was French and at first he did not preach often in English, as he still lacked mastery of that language. But gradually his command of English improved and opportunities to preach in different places arose. His preaching was uncompromisingly evangelistic and often reduced hardened sinners to tears of repentance. But he was most highly regarded for his holy life. He was a godly man.

Wesley once said of him, 'I do not wonder he should be so popular; not only because he preaches with all his might, but because the power of God attends both his preaching and prayer.' John Fletcher was a man filled with the Spirit of God.

Unlike most of Wesley's ordained preachers Fletcher itinerated little, in spite of Wesley's efforts to get him to travel more. Instead, from 1760 he served in the parish of Madeley in Shropshire in the English Midlands. He did minister in nearby parishes on occasions, but not often further afield. He also served for a time as president of Lady Huntingdon's Trevecca College in Wales when it was established in 1768. As this position did not demand his presence fulltime and Madeley was not far from Wales, he was able to continue his ministry in his parish. He eventually resigned from the college over the Arminian/Calvinistic controversy, Fletcher siding with the Wesleys and Arminianism.

Wesley's occasional illnesses made him think of death and caused him to consider who would lead Methodism when he died. His first choice was William Grimshaw, but he died in 1763, many years before Wesley. His next candidate was John Fletcher, 26 years his junior, who seemed the ideal choice. But it was not to be. Fletcher died six years before Wesley.

CHAPTER 21

A QUIETER TIME

Just after Easter 1757 Wesley returned to London and met with the London Society at Spitalfields. The evening gathering attracted 1,200 people. He had expected two of his preachers to come and help him but they did not turn up. He was tired, being 'scarce able to walk or speak', so he decided to wait awhile, but still his helpers did not come. So he 'looked up' to the heavens 'and received strength' and commenced the service without his assistants.

At about 9.30 'God broke in mightily upon the congregation'. The atmosphere was electric. Cries of 'Hallelujah' and 'Praise the Lord' rent the air. Some fell to their knees, praising God; others begged God for forgiveness for their sinfulness. Just about everyone seemed touched by the Spirit of God in some way. It was not something that Wesley had whipped up, rather it was something that God had sent down. When Wesley later returned to his lodgings his tiredness had gone.

He then moved on to the English Midlands. There he met enthusiasm and difficulties. He stopped first in Leicester, where he preached in a building said to hold a thousand people. It was packed and the congregation included about 50 soldiers. Wesley and other early Methodist preachers often seemed keen to minister to soldiers. This was presumably because soldiers often met early death in combat and it was hoped to bring them to Christ before that happened.

It was then on to Birmingham, where he found that many members of the society had become doctrinally confused. He spoke to some of the leaders but his schedule did not permit him to deal with that problem as well as he would have liked. Doctrinal disputes and confusion had become common problems in a number of areas. Methodism was growing rapidly and Wesley had collected around him an army of Methodist preachers covering much of the British Isles, circuit preachers and local preachers. They were varied in shape and size and different in temperament. They came from an array of backgrounds but all had this burning passion to preach Christ and Him crucified. Yet some were not well trained and errors in doctrine were not uncommon.

In Liverpool he found that the society was half the size that it had been. Many had been 'swept away' by a false teacher, who had strongly criticised Wesley's doctrine. Wesley was never a man who put great emphasis on numbers for numbers' sake. He was more than ready to remove people from membership rolls if they proved unfaithful and unwilling to repent. He did not believe in distorting membership figures just to make a good impression.

On 9 May he reached Huddersfield, a manufacturing town in west Yorkshire. It was his first visit to that town. He had encountered troublesome mobs in the past but as he passed through that town's streets he thought 'a wilder people I never saw in England'. These men, women and children seemed just ready 'to devour' Wesley and his travelling companions.

Two years later he preached just outside Huddersfield and things, it seems, had not improved. He recorded that he preached 'to the wildest congregation' that he had seen in Yorkshire. Some shouted and screamed at him and Wesley's helpers had an ongoing fear that suddenly the crowd would erupt into violence. It was a dangerous situation, yet Wesley felt, 'they were restrained by an unseen hand'. In spite of the opposition, he sensed that some in the crowd 'felt the sharpness of God's word'.

England is not noted for having earthquakes, so it was something of a shock when a fairly wide area of western Yorkshire experienced strange rumblings in the middle of May 1757. The ground moved, the walls of houses shook, and crockery and other items fell off shelves. Some people were nearly thrown off their feet with the force of the shaking. This occurred soon after an unusually severe storm, so it understandably, made the people nervous. It seemed as though the elements were against them and perhaps it was all an omen of some future disaster. Was God judging them? Was there worse to come? Was Judgement Day at hand? These concerns, it seems, made them more inclined to listen to a travelling preacher.

The day after the earthquake Wesley preached in the open air in the high-situated village of Heptonstall and it seemed the whole population came out to hear him. Some even climbed on to their roofs to get a better vantage point. As Wesley preached he noticed that it was raining in nearby fields but not on his congregation. He also noted that each person seemed to be listening with deep attention, perhaps encouraged by fears brought about by the terrifying earthquake and storm.

The next day he met William Grimshaw again. This was his territory. Wesley had already preached once that morning and had intended to have a rest during the afternoon but the bold Grimshaw persuaded him to preach at Gawksham in the afternoon, where a congregation assembled on the adjoining hillside.

A few days later Wesley preached in Grimshaw's church in Haworth. A thousand people assembled in the church to take Holy Communion, and such was the crowd of people wishing to hear Wesley that he moved out into the church grounds to preach. This time the weather was not so kind. It rained throughout his sermon.

It was then further north to Whitehaven, Cockermouth and Wigton, and then into Scotland once more. Not for the first time or the last Wesley became lost. He asked a farmer for directions to the host who was expecting them. The farmer sounded confused and the directions he gave proved to be confusing. As Wesley and his companions did their best to follow these directions they became lost, but eventually found themselves at the home of two young women whose father and mother had died, the latter very recently. Wesley, not surprisingly, thought this misdirection providential. He and his helpers prayed with the women and for them and spoke to them of Christ. Wesley left them the next day hoping that 'God will fasten something upon them, which they will not easily shake off.'

That June they visited Dumfries and Thorny Hill in Scotland. On the way they passed the Duke of Queensbury's estate, 'an ancient and noble pile of building, delightfully situated on the side of a pleasant and fruitful hill.' But Wesley reflected that it gave 'no pleasure to its owner; for he does not even behold it with his eyes.' To Wesley this was 'a sore evil. A man has all things and enjoys nothing.'

John Wesley never regarded the rich and the powerful as superior to others nor did he suppose that they were inevitably happy. He always gave respect where it was due but when he mixed with the rich and famous, as at times he did, he always seemed to regard them only as equals, but no more. He was never taken in by wealth, position and power.

An example of this was his relationship with Samuel Johnson, one of the most notable literary figures of the 18th century. Johnson once said that he would be happy to talk to Wesley 'all day and all night too', he found him such delightful company. After one meeting Wesley had with Johnson the preacher rushed off rather abruptly to attend to other responsibilities. Johnson later complained 'the dog [Wesley] enchants you with his conversation and then breaks away to go and visit an old woman. This is very disagreeable to a man who loves to fold his legs and have his talk out as I do.'

What this says about Johnson might be argued but it indicates that Wesley could hold his own amongst the wealthy and intelligent, but was also very comfortable in the presence of the poor. It was a remarkable aspect of a remarkable man.

Another example of this was in connection with an invitation he received from his brother. Charles Wesley and his family were gifted musically. One of his sons later became a well-known composer. On one occasion Charles invited John to a concert put on by these highly talented children. When John arrived at the venue he found a number of Lords and Ladies in the audience. He was not overawed by their presence, but afterwards, he reflected that he loved 'plain company best'.

Ten days after passing the Duke of Queensbury's estate Wesley and an associate were in Kelso. They went to a public place and prepared to preach but no one took any notice of them. Wesley then hit on a brilliant idea. He began to sing one of the Scottish metric Psalms. This, because of its familiarity, attracted attention and very soon at least 15 people 'came within hearing' but kept their distance. They seemed to be nervous about what might follow. Wesley then prayed out loud. When he opened his eyes the congregation had increased considerably, which included, he thought, some of the town's 'chief men'.

He then launched into his sermon as energetically and enthusiastically as if he had been addressing thousands in Bristol. His words 'spared neither rich nor poor'. If the 'chief men' of Kelso were present, he was not going to tailor his message to suit them. After all rich and important though they may have been, in their natural state 'they were but heathens still'. All alike were sinners; all needed the Gospel, and Wesley made sure that they heard it.

He had a similar experience in Wooler the next day. He set up his stand on a street corner to preach and nobody took any notice. He once more sang a Psalm. When he had finished the Psalm a row of children stood before him. They were soon joined by a few adults and Wesley began to preach. By the time he had finished a crowd of about 100 had assembled.

He returned to the south-west of England that August and continued there through September. On this trip he sometimes travelled in a carriage rather than a horse; whether this was because he was a little unwell is unclear. He did not give a reason in his journal. He visited Bristol, Tiverton, St Agnes, Cambourne, St Just, Newlyn and many more towns and villages, preaching as he went. While some of the clergy were still suspicious of him, the people either welcomed him warmly or at least accepted his right to preach in their domain.

At Redruth he preached to a congregation that included 'many' French prisoners. However, it is unlikely that more than a few understood what he said. England's ongoing dispute with France had seen many soldiers on both sides of the conflict taken prisoner. At around the time Wesley was in Cornwall, a hundred poorly-clad British soldiers docked at Penzance. They had been prisoners of the French and were not in a good condition; they were poor in health and dress. A number of them travelled through Redruth on their way back to their respective homes. Remarkably, the people who showed them most kindness as they passed through that region were the French prisoners. These men understood the suffering of their one time enemies.

CHAPTER 22

A NEW DECADE

By the early 1760s Methodism had become well established, particularly in London, Bristol, Cornwall and some parts of the English Midlands and the north. Growth was steady. Wesley was becoming a familiar figure, made striking by his crown of long white hair. But not all ran smoothly. There was still opposition from without and within.

Conflict with George Bell

John Wesley had considerable trouble with one of his associates named George Bell. Bell became a Methodist in 1758 and joined the society at the Foundery, where he was friendly with Thomas Maxfield. It was not long before he began to demonstrate extremes of belief and behaviour. He insisted that he had become perfect, claimed his pronouncements were infallible because they came from the Holy Spirit, denied the necessity of private prayer and claimed that he had healed a number of people. He even later set a date for the return of Christ.

The first time Wesley mentioned Bell in his journal was on 26 December 1761. Here he recorded the words and experience of Mary Special of London. She had hard lumps on her breasts and was in considerable pain. She visited doctors but none could help her. She later attended a prayer meeting run by a Methodist named Daniel Owens. Also in attendance was George Bell. Mary seems to have asked for prayer for healing.

Bell responded, 'Have you faith to be healed?'

She simply said, 'Yes!'

Bell prayed, pronouncing Mary healed by faith, 'and in a moment' all her pain was gone.

The next day the pain returned, though it was less severe. Mary clasped her breasts and prayed 'Lord, if thou wilt, thou canst make me whole.' Immediately the pain went, the lumps vanished, and there was no further relapse, as far as is known, certainly not in the days immediately following.

With such matters John Wesley was cautious but not cynical. He believed that the Lord Jesus healed in New Testament times and there were no good reasons why he could not do so today through His Spirit. Wesley reasoned in his journal, 'Now, here are plain facts: 1/ She was ill; 2/ She is well; 3/ She became so in a moment'. This forced him to ask, 'Which of these can with any modesty be denied?'

In October 1862 Wesley wrote a long and detailed letter to Bell and Owens, which is also recorded in his journal. In it he jotted down which of their beliefs and activities he agreed with and those of which he disapproved. Wesley's main criticisms were that they taught some false teachings and that they were divisive and critical of those who disagreed with them.

He told them, 'I like your doctrine of perfection, or pure love, but I dislike your supposing man may be as perfect as an angel. I dislike you saying, "believe, believe is enough"; that one needs no self-examination, no times of prayer. I like your confidence in God, but I dislike that which has the appearance of pride, of overvaluing yourselves, and undervaluing others. What I most dislike is your littleness of love to your brethren.'

The letter was not unkind but it made clear that in some respects Bell and Owens were not living the Methodist way. As far as Wesley was concerned, they needed to change their ways if they wished to stay under the Methodist banner.

A month later Wesley attended a meeting at which Bell prayed and spoke. Bell prayed for nearly an hour. Wesley admired his 'fervour of spirit', but he did not like the way he screamed almost unintelligibly at times, claimed to be able to discern the spirits and criticised sharply those who disagreed with him. In fact, 'horrid screaming' seems to have been a characteristic of those whom Bell had gathered around him.

A little over a month later Wesley heard Bell speak again. This time Bell did not scream, and though Wesley thought that some of what he said was only from a 'heated imagination', as he said 'nothing dangerously wrong', Wesley did not 'hinder him'. Two weeks later, Wesley heard him yet again. This time he was not pleased. While Wesley did not go into details, there was a hint in his journal that Bell had been critical of Wesley and perhaps others in his prayer. This caused Wesley to state that he did not want Bell praying at the Foundery meetings again.

Yet Wesley did allow him to preach again at the Foundery and at another chapel, as he did not want to act hastily. But after hearing him on these occasions he thought that Bell's efforts were growing 'worse and worse'. According to Wesley, Bell 'spoke as from God, what' he 'knew God had not spoken'.

It is clear that a serious problem had arisen in one of Methodism's major societies. It was made even worse because Thomas Maxfield was also causing trouble at this time, having linked with Bell. In addition, Bell's influence was extending outside London.

But how should Wesley deal with it all? Wesley thought of banning Bell from the Foundery Society but decided instead to try to persuade him to give up his more outrageous views. However, at the beginning of 1763, Bell adopted another controversial idea. He began to teach that the world would end on 28 February that year. Wesley believed that that prediction 'must be false, if the Bible be true.' Therefore Bell was teaching falsity. So Wesley began to preach against this teaching.

However, Wesley did not want to cut Bell off if it could be avoided. Wesley and a couple of associates met Bell and a few of his supporters. Methodism's founder reasoned with Bell, but Bell would not retreat. He was immovable. Early in February he resigned from the Foundery society. Maxfield, whom Wesley now described as 'wrongheaded', also left a couple of months later. They took many supporters with them.

But Bell's influence lingered on. On Monday 28 February, the day Bell had predicted for the end of the world, Wesley preached against Bell's dating of the End. Yet later that evening he noticed that many people, expecting the End to come that night, wandered the fields, afraid to go to their homes. Wesley, untroubled by the prediction, returned to his house, went to bed and was asleep by 10.

Wesley was disappointed at these losses and the trouble surrounding them but not distraught. It would appear from this that Wesley treated Bell fairly. While he certainly criticised and disciplined him, Wesley was also prepared to praise him. He was also patient in his dealings with him.

Gwennap

In September 1765 Wesley was again in Cornwall. One Sunday he preached at St Agnes in the morning and Redruth early in the afternoon. In the evening he went to Gwennap Pit, 'the finest' preaching spot of its type 'in the kingdom'. The crowd that greeted him there was enormous, comprising thousands of people. Wesley estimated that it was as large as any he had seen at Moorfields in London. It was probably the largest assembly he had preached to for some years. Once more pedlars seized their opportunity, having rigged up their stalls near the entrances to the amphitheatre.

Wesley positioned himself at the lowest point in the pit so that his voice could reach the whole vast assembly. He and his helpers sang a hymn. He prayed and then preached on 'Why will ye die?' from Ezekiel

18:31. The crowd was unusually silent as he pressed home that question on the people's consciences. His great voice reached out over the vast throng.

Wesley was aware that his words were striking home in many minds and hearts. True, he could only see clearly the faces of a fraction of the crowd, but he knew that many were listening and understanding his message. When he had concluded the people streamed slowly away. But some stayed behind to speak to him.

A year later he visited Gwennap again. This time an even larger crowd gathered to hear him. The rising slopes on each side were densely packed with people. They listened intently. For most of the time the only sound that could be heard was the voice of John Wesley. Even the wind was silent.

His next visit to Gwennap was in September 1768. He visited the site again 12 months later, and again the following September. In fact, September became his regular time to visit Cornwall. On each occasion a vast throng assembled on the sloping ground (20,000 he thought in 1770) and they listened with rapt attention as Wesley preached. Immediately after that visit he made enquiries of various people as to whether they could hear him at the furthest parts of the venue, yet everybody said that they could. He was by now 67 but his voice was still powerful and in the right environment could be heard at a considerable distance and by thousands of people.

There was one other stunning, though sad, event in September 1770. On the last day of the month George Whitefield died and was buried in the American state of Massachusetts. He was only 55. Put simply, he was worn out from all his travelling and his preaching to vast crowds in Britain and America. He had been the catalyst of major revivals in both countries.

The news took a while to reach Britain, so it was not until 18 November that John Wesley preached his memorial sermon in the chapel in Tottenham Court Road, London, which was later named after White-field. His text was Numbers 23:10: 'Who can count the dust of Jacob, and the number of the fourth part of Israel? Let me die the death of the righteous, and let my last end be like his!'

The chapel was packed and as Wesley entered the pulpit a silence that could be felt embraced the congregation. 'It was an awful season,' recalled Wesley. 'All were still as night. Most appeared to be deeply affected.' Doctrinal and denominational differences were laid aside as one great Christian honoured another great Christian. Whatever friction had existed between them had long disappeared. (When they had last met, 18 months before Whitefield's death, Wesley had recorded 'I had one more agreeable conversation with my old friend and fellow-labourer, George Whitefield.' Whitefield's body, even then, was 'sinking apace' and Wesley suspected that this would be the last time he would meet his old friend on earth.)

Later that day Wesley repeated that memorial sermon at the Tabernacle in Moorfields, and again a few days later in Greenwich. The service in Moorfields was due to start at 5.30 pm, but as the building was full at three, they wisely moved the time forward to 4 pm.

CHAPTER 23

SHOULD A 70-YEAR-OLD SLOW DOWN?

In August 1773 Wesley visited Cornwall again. On Sunday, 22 of that month, Wesley once more preached at Gwennap. He had preached there many times before, usually to massive crowds, but on this occasion even more people had gathered. Not only did they fill the 'pit', but they spilled over into the surrounding area. By his estimate there were 32,000 present.

It was 5 pm when he entered the pit, and as he appeared the crowd hummed with expectation. He climbed on to a small mound near the base of the amphitheatre, raised his hand and the people gradually went quiet.

As usual, Wesley and his helpers sang a hymn to begin. He prayed and then launched into his sermon. In spite of the vast number there was a silence that could be felt as Wesley preached. The only sounds heard were Wesley's voice, an occasional cough, the neighing of a horse, and, towards the end, the sound of people crying.

When he had finished he was exhilarated rather than exhausted. The tiredness would come later. Preaching to vast crowds usually raised his spirits, especially when the people were attentive.

The crowd dispersed slowly. Such a vast number leaving that venue presented problems, so there was some bumping and pushing as the people moved away. Most left but a small number stayed and gathered around Wesley. He spoke to them briefly and invited them back to the Redruth meeting house, where he could deal with them more thoroughly.

In the days immediately following he went on to Cubert, Port Isaac,

Camelford and Launceston in Cornwall, Tiverton in Devon, preaching as he went, and then to Bristol, his second home. If age had slowed him down, it had not done so by much. True, he more often travelled in a carriage now, but his appetite for travelling, preaching and other ministry had not diminished. This was his life. This was his way of serving God.

He was back in Cornwall the following August. On the last day of the month he preached in Redruth. As far as he could tell, nothing remarkable happened during the service, but a few days later he received a note that read:

> The sermon you preached last Thursday evening was, by the grace of God, of great good to my soul. And when you prayed so earnestly for backsliders (of whom I am one) an arrow dipped in blood reached my heart. Ever since I have been resolved never to rest till I find again the rest that remains for the people of God.

When Wesley reached Penzance he reflected that in times past the people in that town were like 'roaring lions', but now they were like 'lambs'. The mood had changed in many places. Where once opposition and threatening behaviour were common, now there was acceptance often mixed with a dose of curiosity.

Early that September he again visited Gwennap and preached to another massive crowd. People converged from many kilometres around to hear him.

In the following days he travelled due east and arrived in London in the middle of October, and for some weeks ministered in that city and the area surrounding it. The following month, he was staying at the Foundery, when he was awoken by a noise. He rose, looked out the window and saw that buildings in a nearby workman's yard were on fire. The wind was also gusting and blowing the flames in the direction of the Foundery. Thoughts of many years ago when he had been dramatically rescued from a fire came to mind.

Soon everybody in the neighbourhood seemed to be awake and in the streets. There were shouts of 'Water! Water!' but the pump would not work. The flames were moving ever closer to the Foundery. Wesley grabbed his papers and other essential items, and praying as he went, escaped into the street.

Suddenly the wind changed. Just as suddenly the pump began to work. Slowly the fire was extinguished and the Foundery was saved.

He next moved in a northerly direction near the eastern coast and came to Yarmouth (aka Great Yarmouth). Yarmouth had once had a flourishing Methodist society but Wesley found that it was now full of discord and confusion. Where once was harmony, 'division after division' disrupted the spirit of the society. Wesley sought to heal the wounds: he counselled, he preached and he exercised discipline.

His sermon was most appropriate. He preached from 1 Corinthians 13:2: 'Though I have all knowledge and all faith, so as to remove mountains, and have not love, it profiteth me nothing.' After that one of the leading figures in that society turned on him and called that 'a damnable doctrine'. Cleary the Yarmouth Methodists had major problems. But, as always, Wesley had a tight schedule and he could not usually stay long in one place, so the next day it was on to Lowestoft, where he found a small but 'lively' society. He was, though, able to make a brief return to Yarmouth that day and this time found its people more responsive.

The Methodists in nearby Norwich were also having major troubles. Sunday preaching had become irregular, many failed to meet in their classes and few took the Lord's Supper. When Wesley arrived there he called the society together, vowing 'to have a regular society or none'. He read the rules that he expected Methodists to live by, emphasising attendance at class meetings and taking the sacrament regularly, and asked them whether they were prepared to keep to these rules or not.

He urged all to attend a meeting the following night who were willing to keep these rules. He also made it clear that he wanted those who were not willing to obey them to stay away. The next night most members of the society went to the meeting. Wesley once more emphasised his 'stick to the rules' approach. After this he reduced the society role from 204 to 174. That night he recorded in his journal, 'And these points shall be carried, if only 50 remain in the society.'

His approach in this instance and in many others was different from how many church leaders operate in the 21st century. He did not judge the health of a Christian group by its size but by its spirituality. While it is true his approach was autocratic, that he took church discipline so seriously is a lesson we can learn.

In March 1775 he once more visited Newcastle in the north. On a cold, blustery evening he preached to a large crowd. One troublemaker kept interrupting Wesley. However, he was stopped by some of the local lads, who grabbed hold of him and stuffed dirt in his mouth. He was silent after that.

Later that year Wesley was taken ill in Ireland. It began with a sore throat, which made it impossible for him to preach. Using one of his pet remedies, he applied 'pounded garlick' to the soles of his feet and the next morning he was much better. However, whether there was any connection between those two events seems unlikely.

Twelve days later he was again unwell. He continued to preach, but sometimes only did so with great difficulty. After one sermon he had a pain in his chest, a weak pulse and was shivering, even though the weather was hot. His condition made it difficult for him to concentrate, which made even reading hard. This seems to have caused him as much concern as the illness itself. He tried to continue on his travels, but he was so weak he eventually had to succumb and go to bed.

He experienced bodily convulsions, his pulse was still weak and his tongue had become swollen and black. He clearly was very ill. Was this the end? He was 72 years of age and had lived the kind of life which would have drained the energy from the strongest. His friends nursed him and prayed for him, but were not optimistic about his recovery. He appeared to be dying.

For more than two days he was unaware of what was going on around him. Then Joseph Bradford, his host, came to him with a cup. 'Sir', he said, 'you must take this'. Wesley had drunk nothing for some time.

Barely conscious, Wesley agreed. Yet the thought went through his mind, 'I will to please him, for it will do me neither harm nor good'. He immediately vomited.

From that moment he began to recover, though slowly at first. The next day he was able to sit up for several hours and walk across the room a number of times. The following day, a Saturday, he sat up for longer and managed to walk across his room 'many times'. On Sunday he was able to go downstairs and sit in the parlour. The following day he was able to take a walk outside and on Tuesday went for a ride in a chaise. On Wednesday, 'trusting in God' and 'to the astonishment' of his friends, he 'set out for Dublin'. That day he travelled 50 kilometres and at the end felt stronger than in the morning. A week later he was preaching again.

***

Methodism had a number of meeting houses and chapels scattered around the country but no central place of worship. After much consideration, it was decided to build a sizable chapel in London's City Road. This new building would thus be in a central position and would replace the aging Foundery. The foundation of the new chapel was laid on 1 April 1777.

On Sunday 1 November 1778, John Wesley presided at the opening of this new chapel. He described it as 'perfectly neat, but not fine' and noted that it could hold many more people than the Foundery. In the morning he preached on Solomon's prayer at the dedication of the Temple in Jerusalem.

Today this same Wesley's Chapel is a place of pilgrimage for Methodists from around the world.

CHAPTER 24

METHODISM ARRIVES IN AMERICA

Methodism arrived in America in the mid-1760s. John and Charles Wesley had, as has been seen, lived there for a period in the 1730s and George Whitefield had visited the country many times since late in that decade. But Wesleyan Methodism as such did not arrive until about 1765.

Like the spread of a number of other such movements, it was not planned initially. It was not a case of John or Charles Wesley despatching a preacher or two to take Methodism across the Atlantic. Rather, individual Methodists migrated to America and took Methodism with them. Only after that did John Wesley send out preachers. It would seem that the first Methodist migrants to America were Irish, which sets the seal in a remarkable way upon Methodist work in Ireland. There is debate over whether the first to arrive settled in Maryland or New York but it was in the latter state that most early progress was made.

The first significant Methodist on the American scene was 'Captain' Thomas Webb. Webb appears to have been born in England and went to America as a soldier in the late 1750s. He lost an eye in battle and was nearly killed. When he left the army, he decided to stay in America, though he did later make a visit back to England, where he was converted and joined the Methodists.

He met John Wesley who appointed him as a local preacher. Wesley described him as 'a man of fire', while Charles Wesley called him an 'honest, zealous, loving enthusiast'. According to John Wesley,

Webb's preaching was not 'deep or regular, yet many flock to hear him'. He was certainly deeply dedicated to Christ. After becoming a local preacher he returned to America taking Methodism with him.

He, with the help of others, built the John Street Methodist Church in New York in 1767, the first specifically Methodist building in America, and acquired another church in Philadelphia for Methodist use. He longed to see Methodism become established in America, but realised that he would need considerable help if that was to be done, so he sent a request to the Methodist Conference in England, asking it to send some preachers across the Atlantic.

The conference met at Leeds early in August 1769. Wesley said of it 'a more loving conference we never had'. It was certainly a very important one. The minutes of that conference recorded that the delegates had received 'a pressing call from our brethren of New York to come over and help them'. The question was then asked, 'Who is willing to go?' Two men, Richard Boardman and Joseph Pilmoor, responded favourably.

Then followed a second question: 'What can we do further in token of our brotherly love?' The response was 'Let us now take a collection among ourselves'. The collection was taken and about £70 was raised for the venture to America.

At that time Boardman had been a Methodist preacher for about six years, Pilmoor, who had been educated at the Methodist School at Kingswood, for four. They left England soon after the conference and arrived in the States late that October.

Upon arrival they received two greetings. The first was from the weather, as a fierce storm marked their entry into Delaware Bay. This storm wrecked a number of other ships in the bay, though their vessel survived. Boardman recorded that in that gale he did not remember having 'one doubt of being eternally saved should the mighty waters swallow us up'. The second greeting was from Captain Webb and a small band of helpers.

Two years later the English conference despatched Francis Asbury to America, and Thomas Rankin and George Shadford followed in 1773. Rankin was a good administrator. Shadford, an ex-soldier, was an ardent evangelist. In that year Rankin was the first man to preside over an American Methodist Conference. The ten men at that conference pledged loyalty to John Wesley and the English Methodist Conference.

Boardman and Pilmoor returned to England in 1774 and Rankin and Shadford in 1778. The rising tensions between America and Britain at this time and the following Revolutionary War (1775-83) made it difficult for Methodist leaders in America. To whom should they be loyal: Britain or America? This was the reason why most went home.

John Wesley wrote a tract to deal with the problems raised by this revolution, called *A Calm Address to our American Colonies*, which was distributed on both sides of the Atlantic. In this document he asked the question 'Has the English Parliament the right to tax the American Colonies?' He answered 'Yes!' The booklet also opposed Republicanism. Calm the address may have been, but it found some enemies at home and it inevitably aroused strong opposition in America. Later he wrote a letter to his American preachers, urging them 'to be peace makers' in that situation and not to align themselves with either side. However, Wesley's *Calm Address* had made it more difficult for them. Because of it many Americans regarded Methodists in America as being disloyal to their country.

Of the early Methodist preachers sent out by the English Conference only Francis Asbury stayed in America. In fact, Asbury is sometimes referred to as the John Wesley of America. Certainly he replicated the work of Wesley in America. He travelled for many years on horseback, visiting numerous scattered towns and settlements and presenting the Gospel to many thousands and pastoring the Methodist societies. He served with great dedication and success.

In the following years, in spite of opposition, Methodism spread further in America in two ways. Firstly, there was additional migration of Methodists from England. Secondly, dedicated itinerant preachers, like Asbury, took the Methodist Gospel far and wide. They rode through rain, snow and burning sun, often facing terrible dangers, such as floods, wild animals and aggressive acts from those who opposed them. They endured great hardships. So evident was their dedication that when the weather turned foul, people would say 'Only crows and Methodist preachers will be out in this weather.'

But this overseas expansion presented John Wesley with a major problem. As has been seen, he was still a priest in the Church of England. He and especially his brother regarded Methodism as part of that church, not distinct from it. This worked in Britain, though with a number of difficulties and tensions, but it was clear that it was never going to work in America. After the Revolutionary War the American Anglican body became a separate Episcopal Church, though with links to the Church of England. American Methodism was never adopted by this Episcopal Church. It was always distinct from it.

***

In August 1783, at the close of the Methodist Conference in England, Wesley was taken ill. In his words, he 'was seized with a most impetuous flux' (diarrhoea), which 'in a few hours was joined by a violent and almost continual cramp: first, in my feet, legs and thighs, then in my side and my throat.' To this was added a fever. The doctor was sent for but his treatment did little good. 'For some days' he became 'worse and worse'. At this time Wesley was ill for about two weeks before he began to improve. After that it was back to work.

As he was, by this time, 80 years of age, he and other Methodist leaders were forced to give thought to what would happen to Methodism after he died. Apart from this illness he was still fit and still able to travel and preach, but it was obvious that he could not go on much longer. With regard to new leaders, William Grimshaw was dead, and though it was unknown at that time, John Fletcher would die in 1785, six years before Wesley. The idea of Methodism led by one man was beginning to fade.

About six months after this illness Wesley executed a Deed of Declaration in the High Court of Chancery to deal with the administration of the Methodist societies and properties after his death. Amongst other matters it named 'the Legal Hundred', that is, 100 preachers who would take leadership of Methodism after he had died. It also made provision for successors when any of the 100 passed away. All power was in the annual conference, operated by those 100 men.

This effectively allowed Methodism to operate as a body separate from the Church of England, though that would not occur in Wesley's lifetime, in Britain at least.

***

As far back as 1775 John Fletcher had urged Wesley to set up an English Methodist Church as a separate body from the Church of England, though retaining some links with the parent body. Included in Fletcher's plan was the idea of ordaining suitable Methodist preachers. While Wesley could see the logic in the idea, his intense loyalty to his church made him hesitate.

In the end, ordaining some of his preachers was forced upon him. By 1784 Methodism in America had grown to nearly 15,000 members. However, it was hindered by a lack of experienced preachers and a lack of ordained men to administer the sacraments. To deal with these problems John Wesley, struggling with his principles, ordained two of his British preachers, Richard Whatcoat and Thomas Vasey, at the beginning of September that year. (In the Church of England only Bishops could ordain and Wesley was not a Bishop.) The Deed of Declaration, the year before, had opened the gates for this.

In the end, Wesley justified these ordinations with the argument that he was 'sending labourers into the harvest'. American Methodism was calling out for preachers and ministers to dispense the sacraments. If he did not ordain such men, then the situation would never improve.

Later that month he sent Whatcoat and Vasey to America, along with Thomas Coke, who had been ordained as an Anglican minister twelve years before. These three men were members of the Legal Hundred. Wesley appointed Coke as the Superintendent of the Methodist Church in the States. It was not long before Coke and Francis Asbury were made Bishops of the newly-named Methodist Episcopal Church in America. But this was a step too far for John Wesley. He was not pleased by this move. He wrote to Asbury asking, 'How can you, how dare you suffer yourself to be called Bishop? I shudder, I start at the very thought. No one by my consent shall ever call me Bishop. For my sake, for God's sake, for Christ's sake put a full end to this.' But American Methodism was already moving out of his control.

Charles Wesley was also displeased, initially about John ordaining these preachers. That news shocked him. Charles sent a letter to his brother, pleading with him to reconsider his actions, but it was too late, and anyway brother John had thought the issue through and had no intention of changing his mind. American Methodism needed ordained men, so he ordained them and did not regret it.

In the years ahead, John Wesley ordained more of his preachers, some for ministry in Britain, others for overseas.

CHAPTER 25

THE LATER YEARS

By the 1780s John Wesley had become not just a familiar figure through-out the British Isles, but, for the most part, a popular one. His flowing, white hair made him instantly recognisable. His amiable manner made him warmly welcomed. He continued his systematic travels, preaching as he went, and crowds came to hear him. His travels had long since been conducted to a plan. Every two years he went through Great Britain and Ireland, preaching and caring for the societies. In doing so, he travelled up to 8,000 kilometres a year, sometimes on horseback and sometimes in a carriage. It was a demanding schedule but one that he was physically and mentally able to carry out.

In one town he visited, every house he entered was suddenly filled with people, asking him to pray for them. Opposition had not entirely dis-appeared but there was much less than in his early days and it was not as fierce as it once had been. Even most of the clergy now accepted him. In sharp contrast to his early ministry, when he was banned from preaching in many places, he was now receiving so many invitations to preach in different churches that he could not accept them all. Often he preached in churches that were packed with people eager to hear him, with more out-side unable to get in. When in Ireland, he was allowed to preach in some Presbyterian churches, in spite of the doctrinal differences.

On one occasion, he was even invited to dine with 'his old opponent' Bishop Lavington of Exeter. Lavington had fiercely denounced Wesley and Methodism for years, closing pulpits to Methodist preachers and writing pamphlets attacking the movement. But in the final years of his life he became much more favourably disposed towards it.

In the summer of 1780 at Newark-on-Trent in the north of England Wesley was preaching to a crowd of over 2,000 when a large, drunken man became 'very noisy and turbulent'. For a while it seemed as though he might drown out Wesley's voice. Certainly he was an unwanted distraction. Suddenly an almost-as-large woman burst onto the scene. It was the man's wife. Wesley called her 'the bravest Amazon of her race'. She grabbed the man by the collar, bashed him a couple of times and dragged him away, cursing as she went. As they reached the edge of the crowd, Wesley seized the opportunity and continued his sermon uninterrupted. The man later rejoined the congregation and 'stood as quiet as a lamb'.

A couple of months later Wesley was preaching to a substantial audience in Penzance, in Cornwall, where a company of soldiers was billeted. As Wesley was speaking, the soldiers suddenly appeared, led by their officer. The officer ordered his men to march through the crowd, which opened up, like a door on its hinges, to make way for them. Once they had passed through the crowd closed up again and Wesley continued preaching. The soldiers marched on.

Also that summer he travelled with his brother to Bath in the southwest and found some divisions in the large society there. The two Wesleys interviewed as many society members as they could and urged unity. By the time the brothers left they sensed a slight improvement and a few people were even added to the society. John thought it necessary to return a few days later to make sure the improvement continued.

There was also trouble in Colchester in Essex. Some of the class leaders had died and others were neglecting their responsibilities, leaving the people virtually leaderless. Also, some services had been cancelled and others were sparsely attended. Wesley was not pleased. He regarded it as a society in decay. He went there hoping 'to strengthen the things which remained, that were ready to die.' When it was announced that he would be preaching, a large body of people assembled to hear him. He preached on 'the terrors of the Lord.' Wesley was never afraid to preach about God's judgement and hell. This sermon shook them.

The next day Wesley began to visit different members of the society, on the lookout for new class leaders. He found some that he considered suitable and left that society in a better condition than he had found it. Some months later he returned and made some further adjustments to the classes to make them more effective.

At around this time he had another dangerous experience at sea. He and five friends went to Liverpool to catch a vessel to Ireland. When they arrived, they found an available boat but the winds were too strong for it to sail, so they could do nothing but wait. Sooner than expected, the captain came to tell them that the wind had abated and that they would sail soon. The six Methodists boarded the vessel and it set out to sea.

It was not long before the wind increased in intensity. The ship pitched and tossed violently. While not terrified, as he had been on his trip to America, Wesley nonetheless had a bad bout of seasickness. In addition, the turbulent waves sent him crashing into the side of the ship and furniture, badly bruising him.

If this was not enough, the preachers' horses below decks panicked. They neighed loudly in terror and kicked the sides of the vessel. So wild was their behaviour, that it seemed likely that they might seriously damage the boat.

The situation was perilous. Faced with this dreadful predicament, the boat's captain approached Wesley. 'Mr Wesley, Your horses are putting us all in danger. I think we might have to slaughter them.' The roaring of the wind and the violent sounds coming from the horses produced an ominous emphasis upon his words.

Wesley hesitated before giving his reply. Then he said, 'You may be right, captain, but I'm reluctant to do it. I'll discuss it with my associates.'

So Wesley discussed it with his companions. Before they had reached a decision, the horses quietened down, making such drastic action unnecessary.

Wesley and his friends prayed. After two days and nights of enduring these appalling conditions, the ship limped into Holyhead harbour. John Wesley then wisely decided it was not God's will for him to go to Ireland at that time.

There was also danger on land, even in the home. Once, when he was the guest in the residence of a Dr Douglas, he was going down the stairs from his bedroom when the carpet slipped from under his feet and he fell head first down six or seven stairs. In the fall his 'head rebounded once or twice from the edge of the stone stairs'. His concerned host quickly came to his aid, but Wesley rose from the floor 'as well as ever', with only minor injuries to two of his fingers. He later recorded in his Journal, that his landing felt 'as if I had fallen on a cushion or a pillow'. Yet it was unlikely to have been that soft and Wesley knew that this was just another example of God's protecting hand.

Dangers also existed on the roads. On one visit in the south-west, Wesley was warned that some highwaymen were robbing travellers in the region he was moving through. But he felt 'no uneasiness' about it and carried on with his journey. He believed that God would protect him. When he arrived at his destination unmolested, he learned that the robbers had been captured by the authorities. As Wesley often said, 'Doth not God give his angels charge over us to keep us in all our ways?'

At the close of 1784 Wesley was allowed to preach at Newgate Prison, which once had been closed to him. He was given the opportunity of preaching to all the inmates, 47 of whom were under the death sentence.

As the prisoners entered the room where Wesley was to speak, 'the clink of their chains' struck him as being 'very awful'. Wesley preached on 'There is joy in heaven over one sinner that repenteth'. (Luke 15:7)

The prisoners listened in silence, apart from the continued noise of their chains as they moved. By the end of his sermon many of the prisoners were reduced to tears and Wesley believed that some found peace in Christ at that time. A few days later twenty of them were executed, including five whom Wesley thought had been born again.

It had been a common practice for his London society to distribute coal and food to the poor early in winter. However, at the beginning of 1786 Wesley realised that they were not doing enough for those in need, so he spent four days traipsing through the snow-covered London streets, visiting people and begging for money so that he could help the less fortunate.

There were times in the 1780s when his voice failed him, but not often. When this did happen it was usually at the end of a sermon. In most cases he was able to travel and preach without difficulty and without weariness.

He still at times attracted massive crowds. In July 1781 he preached to 'thousands upon thousands' at Bradford in Yorkshire. That September he proclaimed the word to 22,000 at Gwennap, and when he returned there the following year many thousands again heard him. One morning in April 1784 he spoke to 'a huge congregation' in Manchester and later that day to 'a far larger' one in the same city.

***

In the 1780s two major Methodists died. Towards the end of 1785 there was an outbreak of typhoid in the Shropshire town of Madeley. John Fletcher, whose health had not been good for some time, caught the disease and died. Wesley preached the funeral sermon for his long-time friend in London on 6 November.

On 29 March 1788 Charles Wesley died. He and his family had settled in the London borough of Marylebone, and he was buried in the local parish church, not in the grounds of Wesley's Chapel, as John had hoped. Shortly before he died he told his parish minister, 'I have lived and I die a member of the Church of England. I pray you bury me in your churchyard.' Charles was an Anglican first and a Methodist second. Yet the relationship between the two brothers had remained good, in spite of disagreements. The younger Wesley will live forever through his many wonderful hymns.

CHAPTER 26

WESLEY'S SOCIAL CONSCIENCE

John Wesley's aim was to spread scriptural holiness throughout the land. It was not enough to bring people to Christ; converts needed to live holy lives, as Wesley, in God's strength, tried to do. He believed that the Bible taught not only individual salvation and a personal relationship with God, but also honesty, integrity, compassion and social justice. These were important issues for him. One aspect of this holiness evident in his life was that he had a strong social conscience.

One major stand he took in this regard was his opposition to smuggling. In a number of coastal areas of England smuggling was commonplace. This practice had become widespread in the 18th century by those wishing to avoid government taxation on imported goods. It was estimated that in one south-eastern county 4,000 horses were used in the trade. But it was illegal.

Wesley became disturbed when he found some of his people involved in it. He quickly learned that because someone bore the label 'Methodist' it did not mean that they would live the life that he expected of them. Some Methodists smuggled goods, while others were quite happy to reap benefit from trading in those goods. But Wesley believed Christians should pay their taxes and not cheat the system. To Wesley smugglers were 'robbers'.

In 1753 at a meeting of a major Cornish society he was shocked to discover that most members in that society were benefitting from smuggling in one way or another. Wesley set aside all other business at that meeting and focussed on that issue. He told them that if they did not stop smuggling he would sever connection with them.

In June 1757 he told the members of the society in Sunderland in the north of England that he would not tolerate their dealing in smuggled goods. Yet some society members refused to give up the practice, so he removed them from the roll.

Early in 1767 Wesley wrote a pamphlet called *A Word to a Smuggler*, in which he argued against all types of involvement in smuggling, direct or indirect. To Wesley, smuggling was the same as the 'picking of pockets'. He quoted Jesus' words 'Render unto Caesar the things that are Caesar's, and unto God the things that are God's'. (Mathew 22:21) As the tax due on the smuggled items was the legitimate income of a modern Caesar, King George, then to deliberately avoid paying it was to disobey Christ. 'Be as exact in giving the King what is due to the King,' he said, 'as in giving God what is due to God'.

In addition Wesley argued 'King George is the father of all his subjects'. To deliberately avoid paying tax to him was like robbing 'a good father'. Wesley also pointed out that if many people avoided paying tax, then an extra tax burden would fall upon those who did because of the shortfall. John Wesley believed that Methodists, indeed, any Christians, should be honest citizens, and they should pay their way.

Wesley was also strongly opposed to the slave trade, particularly in his later years. In the middle of 1755 and again in 1756 Wesley received letters from a minister in Virginia in America, drawing his attention to the spiritual condition of the African slaves in that state. This man estimated that half the state's population were slaves and that their spiritual welfare was generally completely ignored. Yet about 300 of them attended his church and most showed great interest in the Gospel. He seemed surprised when a large number of them desired baptism, and after he had checked on their spiritual condition and instructed them, about 100 were baptised. The minister in a neighbouring church also found the Africans open to the Gospel and experienced similar results.

Wesley's American correspondent observed that generally the slave owners were not interested in the intellectual and spiritual welfare of their slaves. Yet he noted that some slaves had learned to read and he supplied books for them, though they were never enough. He also noted that they had 'the nicest ear for music' and loved to sing God's praises.

It appears that Wesley sent the minister some more books, which were gratefully received. They were distributed amongst both the white and African people. The slaves were especially fond of the hymn books and at times used them to sing long into the night. This is not to say that all the slaves were interested but many in that neighbourhood were.

John Wesley thought this information important enough to include large parts of these letters in his Journal. They were presumably foundation stones of his opposition to slavery.

In 1774 he wrote a pamphlet titled *Thoughts upon Slavery*. In it he criticised the slave trade and slave holding in strong terms, and he did not omit Britain from his critical comments. He criticised the long hours slaves were made to work and the terrible punishments inflicted upon them. In British colonies in the West Indies, for example, 'they work from daybreak to noon, and from two o'clock until dark'. Many were 'whipped most unmercifully' so that their bodies are 'long after wealed and scarred usually from the shoulders to the waist'. In this booklet Wesley said that 'slave-holding' is never consistent 'with any degree of natural justice' and 'is utterly inconsistent with mercy'.

He also penned anti-slavery comments in his *Calm Address to our American Colonies*, written in 1775. But his anti-slavery stand became its most effective near the end of his life. He became a keen supporter of those engaged in trying to rid the world of slavery.

To that end, on 11 October 1787 he wrote a letter of support to Granville Sharp, an abolitionist. Sharp was a civil servant who was the chairman of the recently established Society for Effecting the Abolition of the Slave Trade.

At the end of February 1791, Wesley, a few days before he died, wrote an encouraging letter to William Wilberforce. In it he called slavery an 'execrable villainy, which is the scandal of religion, England and human nature.' He urged Wilberforce not to 'weary in well doing'. He warned him, though, that 'Unless God' had raised him up for this task, he would be 'worn out by the opposition of men and devils. "But if God be for you, who can be against you?" Are all of them stronger than God?' Wesley knew that the way ahead for Wilberforce would not be easy, and it wasn't. But, he urged Wilberforce to 'Go on in the name of God and in the power of his might, till even American slavery shall vanish away before it.' At the end of his letter Wesley prayed 'That He who has guided you from your youth up, may continue to strengthen you in this and all things'. Wilberforce needed that guidance and strength, and he received it in his great work.

CHAPTER 27

WESLEY'S LAST DAYS

Approaching the age of 80, John Wesley was still in remarkably good health, with a surprising amount of energy and willingness to work. In 1782 he said, 'I entered my eightieth year, but, blessed be God, my time is not "labour and sorrow". I find no more pain or bodily infirmities than at five-and-twenty. This I still impute to the power of God, fitting me for what he calls me to; to my still travelling four to five thousand miles a year; to my sleeping, night or day, whenever I want it; to my rising at a set hour; and to my constant preaching, particularly in the morning.'

That a man of those years could continue such a demanding lifestyle is remarkable. It was almost miraculous.

However, by the first day of 1790 age had caught up with him. The 86-year-old Wesley then said, 'I am now an old man, decayed from head to foot. My eyes are dim; my right hand shakes much; my mouth is hot and dry every morning; I have a lingering fever almost every day; my motion is weak and slow.' Yet he could still rejoice in God, because 'I do not slack my labour; I can preach and write still.' Old age and the infirmities that come with it did not stop him taking the Gospel to others.

One acquaintance was deeply struck by Wesley's appearance and demeanour in his old age. He observed, 'So fine an old man I never saw! The happiness of his mind beamed forth in his countenance.'

On 2 January that year he preached to a large congregation at

Snowfields. The next day, a Sunday, he led the covenant service at the new chapel in London, with 'nearly 2,000 in attendance. At the end of the month he began meeting the members of the London classes, which took a week. In February he held a service especially for children in the West Street Chapel. The children 'flocked together from every quarter and surely God was in the midst of them'. Wesley spoke on 'Come, ye little children, hearken unto me; and I will teach you the fear of the Lord'. (Psalm 34:11)

Wesley related well to children. On one occasion a few years earlier he had preached in Oldham in the north. Before the service hundreds of children lined the streets intent on seeing him. Afterwards they crowded around him and would not go away until he shook the hand of each child. Yet he did not usually find children's ministry easy.

Over the years a number of artists had painted portraits or produced busts of Wesley. Towards the end of February he once more sat to have his portrait painted. He seemed surprised that anyone would want a picture of someone his age. In the next century many replica busts of Wesley were produced for the Methodist faithful. As Methodism became strong in the area of the Staffordshire potteries, the supply of these busts seemed endless.

In March he travelled west to Bristol and found 'a people ready prepared for the Lord'. He was impressed with their earnestness. Yet he grieved that the Bristol society had ceased to grow. He then proceeded north to Birmingham and on to Wednesbury, Madeley, Manchester, Warrington and 'wicked' Wigan. At the end of May he arrived in Scotland and preached in numerous cities including Aberdeen, Edinburgh and Glasgow.

In most of these places Wesley preached indoors, though on occasions the size of the crowd forced him outdoors. Preaching to massive outdoor crowds, as he had done so often in earlier years, was now beyond his weakening voice and strength. Yet his age did not stop him travelling, nor did it stop him preaching. In those three months he had journeyed from London to Bristol in the south-west, on to the Midlands, north through Lancashire and Yorkshire, and then to Scotland, preaching as he went. He still had remarkable energy for a man nearing 87 and he had retained his great dedication and determination. Nothing would stop him but death or a complete breakdown in his physical powers. Yet could they be far away?

Returning south, he preached in the Essex town of Colchester on 11 October. The large congregation included rich and poor, staunch Methodists and representatives from a number of local churches. By this time he was so feeble that two of his preachers stood one on either side of him, holding him up as he delivered his message. One man present on the occasion recalled years later, 'His feeble voice was barely audible; but his reverend countenance, especially his long white locks, formed a picture never to be forgotten. It was for the most part a pantomime, but the pantomime went to the heart. I never saw anything comparable to it in later life.' Clearly Wesley's physical powers were sharply declining but his appeal was not.

On 24 October 1790 he recorded in his journal 'I explained to a numerous congregation in Spitalfields Church "the whole armour of God". St Paul's, Shadwell, was still more crowded in the afternoon, while I enforced that important truth, "One thing is needful"; and I hope many, even then, resolved to choose the better part.'

After that the journal fell silent, yet his voice did not. He continued to preach through to the first two months of 1791, but only in the London area. He was now too frail to travel any further. From that time his voice was no longer heard in public. He spent his final few days in his home in London's City Road, drifting in and out of sleep.

His friends, relatives and colleagues gathered around him, including Sally Wesley, the widow of Charles. He slept. Some friends left, others came. There was always someone with him. After one disturbed night, to everyone's surprise he burst forth into song, singing one of his brother's hymns:

All glory to God in the sky,
and peace upon earth be restored!
O Jesus, exalted on high,
Appear, our omnipotent Lord!
Who, meanly in Bethlehem born,
Didst stoop to redeem a lost race.
Once more to thy people return,
And reign in thy Kingdom of grace.

But the effort was too much for him. He fell back on his pillow, exhausted. Later that day he was helped into a chair and he sat there quietly.

After that, speaking became more and more difficult. The voice that had thrilled many thousands for over 50 years could barely utter a sound. Yet suddenly he cried out, 'The best of all is, God is with us.' He raised his frail right arm and repeated in a louder voice, 'The best of all is, God is with us.' But his strength was spent, and he sank back into his bed once more.

A day or two later, on the morning of 2 March 1791, John Wesley muttered 'Farewell!' groaned and died.

Six days after his death, his body was laid near the entrance of the City Road Chapel. Thousands came to pay tribute to him. The next day he was buried in the chapel grounds, on the other side of the road from where his mother was buried. Before his death he had instructed his followers that at his funeral he wanted 'no hearse, no coach, no pomp, except the tears of them that loved me and are following me to Abraham's bosom.' In that, John Wesley got what he wanted. No pomp, but the tears of those that loved him flowed.

***

In John Wesley's over 50 years of ministry he travelled by horse and by carriage not less than 300,000 kilometres, preached to hundreds of thousands, counselled thousands individually, read hundreds of books, wrote hundreds of letters and numerous books, led Methodist Conferences and engaged in conversation with the lowly and the mighty. That one man could do all this is, in itself, outstanding. That he could do it with such remarkable, positive results is even more so. He served God with great energy and dedication, and God mightily blessed his ministry. Indeed, the results that emerged from his labour were not just because of human effort, but because of that divine blessing.

Wesley was always a careful user of time. He once said, 'Though I am always in haste, I am never in a hurry, because I never take on any more work than I can get through with perfect calmness of spirit.' Yet his workload was more than enough for two men.

When he died there were well over 70,000 men and women registered in Methodist societies in Britain. There were another 43,000 or more in America, and over 5,000 in overseas Methodist missions. Many of these men and women had been converted from virtual heathenism. But even those figures do not fully reflect Wesley's influence. There were many others who, while converted through Methodist ministry, did not join Methodism. He also influenced many clergy of the Church of England who did not ally themselves with the Methodist cause, and the clergy of other denominations. It is also no coincidence that the modern missionary movement began soon after Wesley's death. Wesley had kindled the fires that made that possible.

Many tributes have been paid to Wesley in his time and since. Sally Wesley, the wife of Charles, described John as being 'born with a temper which scarcely any injuries could provoke, ingratitude ruffle or contradic-

David Malcolm Bennett

169

tions weary. His gentleness and forbearance rendered him so much the object of love amongst the people who placed themselves under his care that they considered "their sovereign pastor as a sovereign good".' That is a powerful tribute to him as a person from one who knew him well.

The *Gentleman's Magazine* said that Wesley had done 'infinite good to the lower classes of people', and it went on to describe him as 'one of the few characters who outlived enmity and prejudice, and received in his later years every mark of esteem from every denomination.' Augustine Birrell (1850-1933), a politician and writer, called him 'the greatest force of the eighteenth century'. Sir Charles Grant Robertson (1869-1944), a historian and academic, called him 'the most striking of eighteenth-century figures'. Certainly there could have been few in his time who had greater influence over such a vast number, and there were probably none who had personal contact with so many people.

It is also sometimes said that the Evangelical Revival of the 18th century, spearheaded by John Wesley, saved Britain from the terrors of a revolution such as the one that hit France at the end of that century. While this may be an exaggeration, there is some justification for believing that Britain had a more gradual, but generally peaceful, 'revolution' in the 19th century because of that revival.

In 2002 the BBC conducted a poll searching for the hundred greatest Britons ever. That is, the greatest Britons in all ages, in all fields of endeavour. Even though this poll was conducted in a secular age and the votes seem to have favoured 20th century figures, John Wesley was ranked in 50th position.

CHAPTER 28

WESLEY'S LEGACY

British Methodism

While John Wesley's influence went well beyond Methodism, in that he had influence directly and indirectly upon people in other denominations and in society generally, Methodism was his main legacy.

In the period after Wesley's death British Methodism separated from the Church of England. This had always seemed inevitable. Methodism also grew dramatically. In the 70 years after John Wesley died Methodism underwent two seemingly opposing experiences: it divided and it multiplied. Though it divided into several factions, its numbers increased considerably. Long before the end of the 19th century these various Methodist groups contained in total more members than any other Christian denomination in England and Wales except the Church of England.

Division

The groups that broke away from the main (Wesleyan Methodist) body adopted various names, but nearly always used the terms Methodist or Wesleyan within those names. For example, the first of the movements to break away was the Methodist New Connexion, which left as early as 1797, a mere six years after the death of John Wesley. This defection was due to the desire of some in the movement for lay participation at the annual conference. The New Connexion was never a large group.

More important and certainly larger, was the Primitive Methodist Church, 'the Prims'. This denomination emerged in 1811 after a dispute amongst the Wesleyan Methodists about holding American-styled camp meetings. It was mainly a working class church and grew rapidly.

Then there were the Methodist or Wesleyan Reformers, who emerged in the early 1850s. In this movement about 100,000 broke away from the main body, not in an organised movement but in a disconnected fashion. Their main grievance was the perceived autocracy of the Wesleyan leadership. Many of the Reformers either fell into slack, disorganised methods, or fell into the same autocratic errors that they were fleeing from. Most of the Reformers later joined with other breakaway Methodist groups.

Other Methodist denominations in Britain during the 19th century included the Bible Christians, the Tent Methodists, the Independent Methodists and the Wesleyan Methodist Association.

Growth

With the onset of the Industrial Revolution and the resulting massive population movements, the parochial structures of the Church of England proved inadequate to cope. For example, mid-century there were no less than 12 London Anglican parishes with a population in excess of 25,000, while in Bradford one parish had over 75,000 people. In addition, in country districts the Church of England was often controlled by the local gentry and not surprisingly the poorer people in those communities frequently preferred to look elsewhere for their spiritual support.

What the Established Church could not provide, Methodism could, and this was one of the reasons for its growth in the years after Wesley. In theory, and often in practice, a farm hand or a miner could rise to become a Methodist local preacher, and so carry out considerable and effective work for the Kingdom of God, which he would be unable to do in the Church of England.

While there is no doubt that Methodism gained members because of the practical problems experienced by the Church of England, it would be a big mistake to assume that all its gains were from this cause. Methodism's increases in the 19th century were massive and cannot be due only to social issues. According to the 1851 census, Wesleyan Methodists chapels alone grew from 825 in 1801 to an astonishing 11,007 a mere 50 years later, and the total attendance at all services increased from 165,000 to 2,194,298. That is, both increased by a multiple of over 13 times in half a century against a population that only doubled in that time. The Wesleyans grew at six times the rate of the population.

The Primitive Methodists, who only broke away from the parent body in 1811, had 1,555 chapels by 1850 and 3,585 two decades later. That growth from a handful of discontented but enthusiastic Christians in 1811 to over 1,500 chapels 40 years later is staggering. Then in the next 20 years, they more than doubled their number of chapels, but the population in that time only grew by a quarter.

Such large increases strongly suggest that there was a major revival or revivals in the first 70 years of the 19th century, into which John Wesley's Methodism was ideally equipped to tap. By 1883 the membership in all British churches in the Methodist tradition totalled 788,702.

The main British Methodist bodies united in 1932 to form the Methodist Church of Great Britain and Northern Ireland, which is still a major non-conformist church today. Consideration was given to re-joining the Church of England in the 1960s, but the Methodist Conference decided against it.

Methodism in Other Lands

As has been seen, Methodism arrived in America early. What is more, it grew rapidly and the Methodist Episcopal Church became one of the largest American denominations and the major force in world Methodism. As in Britain, smaller groups broke away from the main body, but usually retained a Methodist identity. Three major American Methodist denominations united in 1939 to form 'The Methodist Church' and another church joined them in 1968 to make 'The United Methodist Church', the largest Methodist denomination in the world.

Methodism has reached every continent, and apart from America, is especially strong in parts of Africa and the Caribbean and Pacific Islands, most particularly Fiji and Tonga.

The Methodist bodies of some nations and regions have united with other non-Methodist denominations to present a more united front. For example, the Methodist Church of Australia joined with many Presbyterian and Congregationalist congregations in 1977 to form the Uniting Church of Australia. Another is the Church of South India, formed in 1947, which is made up of churches that were originally Anglican, Methodist, Presbyterian and Congregationalist.

John Wesley's Methodism is truly a worldwide faith.

Also available from David Malcolm Bennett

From Ashes to Glory

ISBN: 978-1-921632-76-1
$18.99 paperback
Release date: 1 March 2014
Joint Winner of the 2014 CALEB Award:
Biography category

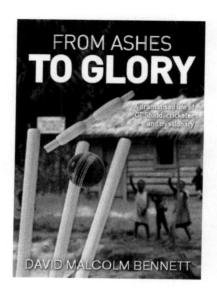

A Dramaticised retelling of CT Studd, his cricket, his mission work and the decisions he made which helped form the mission organisation WEC International.

CT (Charlie) Studd was a cricketer of the highest class. He played in the famed Test Match between England and Australia in 1882 that began the legend of the Ashes. From Ashes to Glory tells the story of this remarkable, dedicated man, and contains an authentic account of the 1882 Ashes Test, with all its drama.

At the peak of his fame Studd retired from cricket to serve as a missionary in China. In 1885 he was one of seven men of wealth and privilege ('The Cambridge Seven'), who shocked the nation, by giving up everything to take the Gospel of Jesus Christ to the Chinese. While there he suffered much, but saw many people come to Christ. He later spent six years as a missionary in India, where he opened a school which is still serving the community today.

CPSIA information can be obtained
at www.ICGtesting.com
Printed in the USA
BVHW06s0513230418
513860BV00001B/90/P

9 781925 139273